Pluralism

The World of Political Science—
The development of the discipline

Book series edited by
Michael Stein and John Trent

Professors **Michael B. Stein** and **John E. Trent** are the co-editors of the book series "The World of Political Science". The former is professor of Political Science at McMaster University in Hamilton, Ontario, Canada. The latter is a Fellow in the Center of Governance of the University of Ottawa, in Ottawa, Ontario, Canada, and a former professor in its Department of Political science.

Dr.**Tim Heinmiller** is the coordinator of the series, and Assistant Professor of Political Science at Brock University in St. Catherines, Ontario, Canada.

Rainer Eisfeld (ed.)

Pluralism
Developments in the Theory and Practice
of Democracy

Barbara Budrich Publishers
Opladen & Farmington Hills 2006

A CIP catalogue record for this book is available from
Die Deutsche Bibliothek (The German Library)

© 2006 by Barbara Budrich Publishers, Opladen
    www.barbara-budrich.net
    ISBN 10   **3-86649-028-3 (paperback)**
    ISBN 13   **978-3-86649-028-4 (paperback)**

Die Deutsche Bibliothek – CIP-Einheitsaufnahme
Ein Titeldatensatz für die Publikation ist bei Der Deutschen Bibliothek erhältlich.

Verlag Barbara Budrich ⓑ Barbara Budrich Publishers
Stauffenbergstr. 7. D-51379 Leverkusen Opladen, Germany

28347 Ridgebrook. Farmington Hills, MI 48334. USA
www.barbara-budrich.net

Jacket illustration by disegno, Wuppertal, Germany – www.disenjo.de
Printed in Europe on acid-free paper by
Paper & Tinta, Poland

Contents

Foreword 7

Preface 9

Introduction
Rainer Eisfeld 11

The Plural Forms of Pluralism
Theodore J. Lowi 21

Pluralism and Democratic Governance:
A Century of Changing Research Frameworks
Rainer Eisfeld 39

Pluralism and the Politics of Diversity
Avigail Eisenberg 59

Plurality, Pluralism and Power: Elements of Pluralist
Analysis in an Age of Globalization
Philip G. Cerny 81

Bibliography 111

Index 123

Foreword

This is the fourth volume in "The World of Political Science" book series sponsored by Research Committee 33 on the Study of Political Science as a Discipline, one of about 50 Research Committees of the International Political Science Association (IPSA). Each volume of the series is being prepared by leading international scholars representing one of the research committees of IPSA. We expect to publish at least one more volume in the series in the next few months.

"The World of Political Science" series is intended to fulfil several objectives. First, it is international in scope, and includes contributors from all areas of the globe. Second, each volume aims to provide an up-to-date overview of a specific sub-field of political science. Third, although prepared by leading academic specialists, the series is written in a manner which is meant to be accessible both to students of that field and those who want to learn more about it. Fourth, the books offer both a state-of-the-art overview of the sub-fields and an explanation of how these have evolved into what they are today. Thus they serve as part of a broader objective of evaluating the current state of development of political science. Fifth, on the basis of this evaluation, the volume editors and authors will make proposals for the improvement of each sub-field and eventually, for the discipline as a whole.

The fourth volume in the series was authored by members of RC 16 (Socio-Political Pluralism). It is entitled Pluralism: Developments in the Theory and Practice of Democracy. Its major contention is that the theory of pluralism continues to provide a valuable approach to the study and practice of democracy in the twenty-first century, as it did for most of the past century. This argument rests on two assumptions: 1) that political science has as perhaps its major concern the need to secure broad societal participation and representation of social interests in the formulation of public policy, and 2) that political science is also centrally concerned with how to reduce disparities in political resources in order to strengthen the legitimacy of representative and democratic government. It therefore analyzes the concept of pluralism historically since the beginning of the twentieth century from both a descriptive and prescriptive standpoint, and also from a group and individual participatory perspective. Rainer Eisfeld has recruited contributors to this volume from both North America and Europe. They appropriately draw on the diverse and rich theoretical literature on pluralism of these continents for both information and insights.

We also want to express our deep gratitude to Barbara Budrich, the founder and head of Barbara Budrich Publishers, as well as her staff. From the outset, Barbara has been the person on the publication side most responsible for bringing the book series to fruition. She continues to serve as its chief publications manager and promoter. Furthermore, we acknowledge our enormous debt to the Social Science and Humanities Research Council of Canada (SSHRC), whose initial Research Development Initiatives Grant #820-1999-1022 and later extensions made the project possible. In addition, we also pay tribute to IPSA Research Committee 33 on the Study of Political Science as a Discipline and its Project Sub-Committee members, who played a major role in defining the series objectives. The support given by the IPSA Committee on Research and Training to Research Committee 16 on Socio-Political Pluralism in the development of this book has also been essential to the success of the series. Finally, a special word of thanks is owed to our Project Coordinator, Tim Heinmiller, who, as he did with earlier books in the series, has applied his considerable academic and administrative talents to all major concerns of this volume.

As series co-editors, we naturally assume ultimate responsibility for this book series. This project has been a joint and equal collaborative effort on our part right from its beginning, and this has contributed greatly to its success thus far. We also look forward to the future appearance of worthy volumes by other research committees.

Michael Stein (McMaster University)
John Trent (University of Ottawa)

Preface

Citizens' early preparation for civic involvement is not helped by the fact that universities everywhere are suffering from cuts in public funding and ever more conspicuously must rely on private philanthropy.

Needless to say, conveners of research conferences find themselves encumbered by the same financial constraints. The editor and authors are the more indebted to Krzysztof Jasiewicz for organizing, and to Washington and Lee University for hosting, the March 2005 meeting of the International Political Science Association's Research Committee on Socio-Political Pluralism (RC 16), where drafts of the following chapters were discussed.

We would like to thank Christian Leuprecht, Michael Stein and three anonymous peer reviewers for their pertinent comments, and Gabriele Parlmeyer for her care and unflagging patience in formatting and editing the manuscript.

To the members of IPSA RC 16, from whose activities it emerged, this book is gratefully dedicated.

Rainer Eisfeld

Introduction

Pluralism was forged by British thinkers in the early 20th century as a theory focusing on the fundamentally associative character of society, yet striving to reassert the individual's position as the subject of democratic politics. Groups, in other words, were envisaged to operate as instruments, representing individuals rather than replacing them in the political process, thereby *enhancing* chances for individual-centered democracy in a world of increasingly complex socio-political interaction. Political man acting through and in control of his freely established associations: That is the normative vision of pluralism.

As with every representative arrangement, however, in-built tensions remain between original individual interests and eventual group (i.e. leadership) action. To the extent that such group action today has come to be treated as a substitute for individual action in reaching political outcomes, chances for individual-centered democracy are *diminished*. This inference applies the more, because political resources enter the picture as a second pivotal element. Their maldistribution skews the political process, eventually fatally flawing it in favor of powerful minorities. Non-committed or indoctrinated citizens caught in a web of hierarchical organizations: That is often the less than satisfactory (from a democratic theory perspective) reality. Inducing institutional and attitudinal changes remains the main conundrum of pluralism.

Both the vision and the conundrum will resurface in the following pages.

Pluralism originally emerged as an effort to give new meaning to liberal tenets. Classical ("Integral") liberalism in the tradition of John Locke and Adam Smith had "atomized" societal relations. Considering the individual to have precedence, both chronologically and logically, over civil society, the liberal model emphasized the absolute autonomy of freely competing men. "Sinister" factional interests were abhorred, the organization of such interests into permanent associations, especially trade unions, was rejected (Loi Le Chapelier; Combination Acts). "All systems either of preference or of restraint, therefore, being thus completely taken away, the obvious and simple system of natural liberty" – of "liberty, not licence", in Locke's famous words from the *Second Treatise* – "establishes itself of its own accord. Every man, as long as he does not violate the laws of justice, is perfectly left free to pursue his own interest his own way" (Smith 1776: 687).

As liberal maxims became increasingly "detached from any tenable theory of society" (Mills 1963: 189), the work of John Stuart Mill like a seismo-

graph registered both the challenge to principles which liberals had been pro-
pounding and the hesitation to finally reject them. However, Mill definitely
repudiated the liberal ban on trade unions. Although appraising their chances
of generally improving wages and working conditions with a considerable
dose of skepticism, he acknowledged that the individual poor laborer would
be exposed to the dictates of a wealthy employer: "Far from being a hin-
drance to a free market of labor", associations of laborers were "the necessary
instrumentality of that free market" (Mill 1975 [1861]: 563/564, 565).

Obviously, the retrospective diagnosis that "more and more individuals
turned, of necessity, to organization" (Hallowell 1943: 116) not merely referred to workers and trade unions. No other than Mill's contemporary Alexis
de Tocqueville has been credited with observing "that even at the time, 'la
démocratie en Amérique' was a pluralist democracy" (Fraenkel 1964: B 27).
Indeed, Tocqueville's references, under the impression of the Jacksonian
Revolution, to an abundance of voluntary associations, "extemporaneous as-
sembl(ies)" governed by their members' "reason and free will", provided "the
intellectual springboard from which many contemporary thinkers have constructed their own formulations" (Connolly 1969: 4/5).

The French visitor to America, however, also foresaw the decisive contribution of the emerging "large manufacturing establishments" to a new
"inequality of conditions" (Tocqueville 1959: 160/161). When the first pluralists came to argue that liberal individualism had resulted in the "crushing
of individuals ... (of) all but a few" (Follett 1918: 170), the joint-stock company had increasingly commenced replacing the privately owned and managed firm. The divorce between the functions of capital owners and managers
administering shareholders' capital decisively favored both the evolution of
small enterprises into giant corporations and the augmentation in the number
of oligopolistic markets (compare this with Rothschild 1947: 319). The extemporaneous assemblies witnessed by Tocqueville were changing, too,
developing into large-scale farmers', blue collar, white collar and other professional organizations. Governmental interventionism into the economy resulted in ever more formidable administrative bureaucracies: If trade unions,
progressive groups, social democratic and labor parties were pushing governments to assume an active role in stabilizing the economy to prevent cycli-
cal mass unemployment and misery, large corporations, in their "struggle for
position and security" (Rothschild 1947: ibid.) became interested in governmental regulation to "consolidate conditions within various industries"
(Kolko 1963: 287).

Within the framework of a "political capitalism" (Kolko 1963: ibid.) im-
plemented between the wars and increasingly after World War II, business,
labor and farmer associations developed into unequal partners bargaining for
legislative and administrative intervention. The inequality increased as business organization continued to evolve: To step up flexibility, to evade high

wages, encumbering taxes and restrictive monetary policies, nationally based large enterprises spread their subsidiaries over the world, penetrating other economies and changing into multinational corporations in the process (Hymer/Rowthorn 1970: 64, 88). Two decades before the term "globalization" gained currency, it was predicted that the multinational enterprise, without being bound by any "notions of constituency, responsiveness, and account-ability", would reshape world-wide values and behavior patterns, including prevailing perceptions about "the range of possible forms and content that politics may assume" (Osterberg/Ajami 1971: 460, 469).

In a world of national and international blocs, the individual was again relegated to the sidelines. Empirical research on political involvement confirmed widespread individual apathy and alienation existing alongside the institutionalized activities of large associations. In an era characterized by such "notable discontinuities" between "the conditions for an ideal of plural-ism formulated (by Tocqueville) ... and their contemporary equivalents", how could the vision be attained to put back "individual(s) at the center of things" in a fundamentally associative society and polity (Connolly 1969: 5; Laski 1925: 67)?

Between 1915 and 1925, early English pluralists – Harold J. Laski and G. D. H. Cole prominent among them – called for the democratic control of "the various communities of which we are a part" (Mason 1982: IX). Advo-cating the institution of individual self-government ("functional representa-tion") on every social level, they were placing particular emphasis on the workplace, the factory, the enterprise – in short, on industrial democracy. Their concept focused on control, rather than on ownership of the means of production, on the enfranchisement of the citizens (blue and white collar em-ployees) of the political body that was and is the modern enterprise – its proper 'stakeholders' in today's parlance. It became eroded when trade unions, beset by the post-World War I decline in living standards, ceased "hoping to build a better industrial order" and the Labour Party, on its part, favored the sort of nationalizations which, as had early been predicted, "would leave the position of the worker unchanged" (Stears 2002: 268; Wright 1974: 177).

When the notion of pluralism was picked up in the United States a gen-eration later, it gave belated recognition to Arthur F. Bentley's approach (de-veloped even before Laski's and Cole's positions) which essentially reduced human conduct to group action. Individual freedom – and overarching con-sent – were judged to be guaranteed by overlapping group memberships and cross-cutting individual solidarities. Both were supposed to exist in American society as it had emerged from the New Deal reforms. "As everybody knows, in the United States individuals identify with a great diversity of different groups", which "is undoubtedly one of the reasons for the proliferation of bargaining" (Dahl/Lindblom 1953: 329). Even if American pluralism prided itself on being "analytical" rather than "philosophical" (Latham 1952: 9), a more or less explicit normative element was unmistakable. Clearly, the school portrayed ongoing Western democracies (particularly the American variety) "in a favorable light" (Merelman 2003: 50).

Even so, Robert A. Dahl, Charles Lindblom and David B. Truman conceded that political activity, control *and access to government* were determined, to a considerable extent, by income, education and status – in other words, by the position of groups and group leaders in the social structure. The "'cross pressures' of conflicting group loyalties" might result in individual political apathy. Political resources were unequally distributed between business and labor. Capitalist democracies even offered "unusual opportunities" for "pyramiding" such resources into structures of social power and political influence (Truman 1951: 265; Dahl/Lindblom 1953: 315, 329; Dahl 1963: 227). In view of these limitations, two avenues for further theorizing suggested themselves. Both were pursued, starting in the mid-seventies.

One was to unequivocally embrace "realistic" Schumpeterianism, fitting groups into a model of elitist democracy where governments would explicitly privilege the organizations of capital and labor as "partners" in policy-making over associations with weaker political resources; where group leaders would manufacture consent for such policies; and where, consequently, group members would be controlled from above.

Such concepts of liberal or neo-corporatism, as they came to be labeled, were primarily developed in, and focused on, Western Europe after the election of social democratic governments gave more political voice to trade unions during the 1970s and 1980s.

Actually, the divide between liberal pluralism and liberal corporatism was far less pronounced than the more recent approach seemed to imply, considering that the liberal pluralists of the 1950s and 1960s had already singled out moderate, rational conflict "among group leaders, socialized into the dominant values of industrial society", as the demarcation line against radicalism and mass movements (Rogin 1967: 10, 15).

The second alternative consisted in raising the normative question how one might proceed "to achieve the best potentialities of pluralist democracy" by "remedy(ing) the defects of organizational pluralism" (Dahl 1982: 170, 205). This meant conceiving pluralism in terms of a normative concept of democratic transformation such as it had earlier emerged in England. Looking for possible solutions to what "authority in a good society" might be like, Robert Dahl – ever more critical of institutional rigidity, social inequality, and political apathy – suggested "a radical alternative to the American and Soviet status quo", combining industrial self-government and market socialism (id. 1970: 115, 130). Like Harold Laski's concept, the pluralism now expounded by Dahl aimed at a more participatory democracy and an employee-controlled economy. Starting from the premise that unequal social resources will translate into unequal political resources, both Laski's and Dahl's pluralist programs focused on diminishing the discretionary exercise of organizational power *by economically privileged minorities.*

In this volume, it will then be contended that pluralism, as conceptualized by – among others – Laski and Dahl, is still a valid and powerful approach for inquiring into the theory, the practice and the perspectives of 21st century democracy on the following two premises:

1. that the problem of securing broad societal participation – and thus, again, equitable representation of social interests – in the shaping of public policies remains foremost among the concerns addressed by political science, and

2. that reduction of disparities in control over political resources is of prime importance in ensuring the accessibility, accountability, and legitimacy of 'representative' democratic government.

As discussed in the following pages, pluralism emerges as an at once positive (descriptive) and normative (prescriptive) concept. Positively, the concept establishes the existence of a plurality of interests and corresponding social groups which, as latent centers of power, may (and are permitted to) organize into associations. Normatively, it endorses the transformation of this diversity into public policies (which, in turn, are aimed at shaping the social 'order') by a process of group conflict, negotiation and compromise, on condition that basic rights and principles of justice remain respected and protected.

Pluralism, in a nutshell, offers a group *and* a participatory theory – a theory of individual participation by social association in the political process.

While this definition may seem fairly clear-cut, is does not pretend to cover all of the concept's many-faceted meanings. A concept, as explained in the book's first chapter, should not be allowed to remain "frozen" over time against changes in context. Analysis must show that a long-cherished political notion is still serving its purposes in a changing socio-political environment.

Consequently, the first chapter by Theodore J. Lowi, addressing methodological issues, seeks to "unscramble" the concept's complexity and clarify its meaning and context. Lowi resorts to a hypertextual approach for organizing knowledge which he and Mauro Calise first presented half a decade ago: After linking a concept to a number of textual and bibliographical sources for further in-depth analysis, multi-dimensional linkages are developed by placing the core concept in a matrix of logically consistent relationships. Moving "from discrete concepts to relationships between and among concepts" helps to choose contexts, on which the meaning of concepts is apt to depend. This advances the capacity for theory-making (Calise/Lowi 2000: 283, 285).

The choice of concepts, identical to selecting a set of relationships, serves "to expand meaning" and at the same time "to define boundaries" by creating "a clearly structured space". This is definitely a normative endeavor: A core concept, in this case pluralism, is linked "to others most closely associated in the argument one intends to pursue" (ibid.: 293). The concepts deemed necessary in the definition of the core entry provide the intersecting axes of the afore-mentioned matrix, with the core concept placed at the center. By including, in addition to "primary", i.e. central, concepts (the axes), more "secondary" links (called "peripherals"), the four outside corners of the matrix can also be occupied and the scheme be "closed off" (ibid.: 298).

The matrix serves to make choices explicit. Selected concepts – "links in the construction of a theoretical argument" – may "be confronted with, and checked by, other statements" relating to the same given issue. Specific aspects may be criticized and modified. Finally, "new matrices with different cross-tabulations" may be made up (ibid.: 299).

In the matrix, axes and peripherals generate four quadrants, each of which is defined by four concepts. The quadrants provide "property spaces", permitting "to look for four additional derived linkages" – dependent variables characterizing "logical – and substantial – interactions" between the four primary and peripheral links closing off each quadrant (ibid.: 300). In the case of pluralism, the primary concepts chosen for reasons explained in the first chapter are group and class (vertical axis), civil society and government (horizontal axis); the secondary links are party and market (right peripheral), public and community (left peripheral). The property spaces are defined by estate (lower left quadrant), contract (upper left quadrant), coalition (upper right quadrant) and corporation (lower right quadrant) [compare this with figure below, p. 25].

Taking his bibliographical clues from Laski and Bentley, Lowi first delves into what he calls a brief "standard treatment" of the issue, roughly equating pluralism with civil society and political pluralism with civil society-government interaction. Reverting to his systematic approach, he subsequently identifies four types of pluralism: feudal, market-driven, party-driven and, finally, corporate. While the first variety (typified by "estate") may be of merely historical interest, it does provide, as Lowi notes, a bridge between antiquity and modernity which has been slow to crumble in many ways. Capitalism's assault on feudal and post-feudal societies and their mercantilist policies led to the passage from status to contract and to the emergence of market-driven pluralism. Groups, however, in their struggle for position and security (as noted above when referring to the evolution of "political capitalism") again tended to incorporate – make themselves permanent – and to seek public patronage – a "feudal carry-over" that refuses to go away even in the most modern societies.

In the United States at least, even such corporate groups, during the heyday of party pluralism (Type 3, as identified by Lowi), had to accommodate themselves to powerful party "machines" to win access to government. The mediating role of parties declined, however, as interest organizations became more dispersed and entered into direct bargaining with administrations. Because the performance of business – judged by government officials to underlie, rather than being part of, the resulting process of conflict, negotiation and compromise – appears "indispensable" to administrators (Lowi here refers to Lindblom's pertinent analysis), business enjoys a "privileged position". Moving on from Lindblom's assessment, Lowi defines corporate pluralism (Type 4) as the institutionalization of that position: On top of working through interest groups, each corporation "operates as its own interest group, with influence *in* government rather than *on* government".

That, Lowi concludes, "takes pluralism well beyond the group competition and 'bargaining among elites' and party-group coalitions of Type 3". As polyarchy offers no remedy against such "functional feudalism", legitimized in terms of Type 2 and 3 pluralism and "sanitized as partnership", the present pattern should be considered detrimental to democracy.

With pluralism contributing both a claim about reality to political analysis and a normative dimension to democratic theory, Lowi's opening chapter offers a number of guiding insights, viz.: A trip through a conceptual universe is likely to involve a journey through stages of socio-political and economic change. In order to properly denote structures of a specific stage, a concept such as pluralism may require adjectives. If transferred to the present, a notion – in this case, Type 2/3 pluralism – used to describe another historical pattern may be inappropriate for analytical, but perfect for ideological purposes.

It may surprise some readers that Lowi's analysis quite suitably concludes on a line from Tennessee Ernie Ford's famous tune *Sixteen Tons*.

This book's second chapter substantiates and expands on Lowi's results. Rainer Eisfeld reviews a century of pluralist inquiry into how economy, civil society and government have been interacting, and how they should interact, in a democratic polity. For the duration of that period, pluralism has vacillated between diagnosing severe democratic deficits in the process, and accepting the ongoing results of that process. Successive attempts at theory-building left a plethora of debates, without – as the second chapter argues – ever progressing beyond empirical and normative research programs. The general direction which these contending approaches took has been briefly discussed above. The foundations were laid by Bentley in 1908 and by Laski between 1915 and 1925. After that, it became a matter of rediscovery.

Bentley's approach was resuscitated by David B. Truman, to whom it served as "the principal bench mark for (his) thinking" (Truman 1951: IX). Other theorists – such as William Kornhauser, Earl Latham, Lester Milbrath – followed down the same path. Almost simultaneously, Robert Dahl and Charles Lindblom – who "were familiar with the British and European ideas about pluralism" (Dahl 1986: 235) – reintroduced the term for a group-centered approach, explaining that by pluralism they meant "a diversity of social organizations with a large measure of autonomy with respect to one another" as a requirement of polyarchy (Dahl/Lindblom 1953: 302). Chapter 2 goes on to demonstrate how, for a decade and a half, varieties of "liberal" pluralism provided the mainstream paradigm for the analysis of the American and other Western-type political systems; how that paradigm became increasingly subject to criticism on both theoretical and empirical grounds; how, finally, Robert Dahl returned to pluralism the democratizing, "radical" dimension which Harold Laski had first supplied:

"No political democracy can be real that is not as well the reflection of an economic democracy" (Laski 1919b: 38) – "People who are compelled to obey public governments ought to control those governments ... Should this reasoning not apply also to the government of a large economic enterprise?" (Dahl 1982: 184).

The second chapter traces in detail the conceptual evolution sketched out here and earlier in the introduction. It also prepares the ground for a more extensive discussion of two recent developments in the book's following chapters.

The first development concerns the process of economic globalization pushed by both governmental and market players. Diminishing governance capabilities are raising the already institutionalized "privileged" position of business to virtual "veto power" in fiscal, monetary and welfare policies (Ringen 2004: 4). With neo-liberal maxims firmly entrenched, and disparities in control over economic and political resources increasing, social plurality may translate less and less into political pluralism. Or maybe not? Setting out from the tension between plurality and pluralism, the book's concluding chapter – as will be detailed below – looks at how globalization could be reshaping the configuration of interests.

The second development has to do with regional and world-wide migration as part of the globalization process. Basically, it amounts to another conceptual rediscovery over the last decades. During the very period when Harold Laski was arguing in England that only an economic democracy could make political democracy "real", ethnocultural pluralism came to be perceived as "an analogue of political pluralism" in the United States (Menand 2001: 379). Proclaiming a "democracy of nationalities" as the desired goal required that individuals in every ethnic group, rather than being discriminated against by *culturally privileged majorities*, might realize their inherent possibilities according to that group's "spirit and culture" (Kallen 1915: 220). So far, the two debates on political and cultural pluralism have been largely evolving separately. Congruence, however, exists with regard to a politics of inclusion, in the sense that policy-making in pluralist democracies should include, on an equitable basis, as many societal interests as possible.

This raises a number of knotty problems. Are all interests equally amenable to negotiation and compromise? Will interests in an ethnocultural context be perceived by an individual as "contingent", in the sense of expressing more or less perfunctory purposes, or rather as "constitutive" of her/his sense of self? What appears as a neat distinction theoretically, may often become blurred in practice.

To what extent should ethnocultural groups be protected, even supported – for instance, by affirmative action policies? If these groups were conceded collective rights, what effects would such rights have in the case of conflict between groups and (some) members? How, in general, to balance individual against group rights?

These thorny issues are tackled in the third chapter. From a different perspective this time, Avigail Eisenberg once more reviews early English and post-World War II American pluralism. She contrasts voluntary associations and their supposedly "merely" self-interested members, whose purposes are predominantly "instrumental", with ethnocultural "communities" whose members' commitments may run deeper, noting that the American variety of pluralism largely left out the latter. For her further discussion, she draws on the English pluralists' argument that, as a rule, the development of individual capacities is closely interrelated with a rich and democratic "group life". However, these theorists did not really address the question how to balance the role of (ethnocultural) groups with individual well-being if the two should come into conflict. Eisenberg qualifies exclusive reliance on the pretended voluntary character of associations an "illusion" on which theorists of democracy have too often continued to build. Her chapter again highlights the pivotal role which a more equitable distribution of social and political resources would play for an individual's chance to make meaningful choices – choices that might include exiting a group perceived as confining.

Philip G. Cerny, in the final chapter, concurs that the societal base of policymaking is, and will remain, "skewed". He reminds his readers that political systems are not just pluralist or non-pluralist, but rather located on a scale between ideal-type monism at one and ideal-type competitive pluralism at the other end of the spectrum. Cerny joins the book's other authors in pointing out that the transformation of plurality into pluralist practices by group and individual actors requires supportive structural and institutional factors – "a pluralism-generating and pluralism-reinforcing playing field", as he calls it. The process itself will always face contestation – internally by embedded or newly emerging inequalities and clashing values, externally by new claimants who continue to arise nationally and transnationally.

Globalization drastically changes the structures of the playing field. Disaggregating the political process, it replaces the nation-state by multi-level governance (or multi-nodal politics, a term preferred by Cerny). The relationship between plurality and pluralism "becomes more and more complex and problematic": Plurality is augmented, pluralism potentially undermined. With multinational corporations and financial institutions "possessing the lion's share of the kind of resources necessary to pursue their interests" on the new, multilayered, structurally open playing field, the privileged position of business is "dramatically increased". Against an "embedded neoliberalism" (reduction of barriers to trade and cross-border finance, flexibilization of labor markets, transformation of the welfare into the "competition state"), it is becoming "more and more difficult", according to Cerny's analysis, to organize politically effective resistance.

However, this is not quite the whole story. Cerny contends that, because globalization involves pluralization on a number of levels, certainly uneven, but in flux, it opens up, in general terms, new access points and sites for action. The dynamics of that evolution may generate new preferences, new strategies, new – and shifting – coalitions, even opportunities for restructuring the playing field itself. The resulting "pluralism" could certainly remain "locked in" through (partly restructured) economic, social and political hierarchies. It could also, Cerny suggests, add up to a more dynamic process in which group actors "reinvent" themselves in terms of organization and coalition-building and may even succeed in reshaping "the growing institutional plurality".

Political pluralism began as an analytical and a normative project a century ago. The chapters of this book are an attempt to restate that project in terms appropriate to the complexities of a vastly different world. Then as now, a "pluralizing" democracy requires, first and foremost, "resourceful" individuals – meaning, quite literally, individuals committed to pluralist orientations *and* having equitable access to political resources. In the last instance, the uncertain future of pluralism will be determined by a political culture which puts a premium on the educated citizen, prepared and able to involve him- or herself, and consequently on the dispersion – the redistribution, actually – of these resources. To the extent that they maintain democratic practices internally, groups – through the transfer of norms and values – significantly contribute to such a political culture.

To the extent, on the other hand, that groups with democratic practices and involved individuals should become increasingly few in society, solutions to the persistent problem of living democratically will become ever more difficult.

Theodore J. Lowi

The Plural Forms of Pluralism

I. Introduction to the Problem

Unpacking the Concept

Political scientists have a tendency, after having identified a vital problem, of seizing on a conventional ("consensual") concept from the professional vocabulary to represent the phenomenon. Some good may come from this practice, but there are dangers, the greatest of them being intellectual rigidity. This is an aspect of Kuhn's syndrome of conservatism in "normal science" (Kuhn 1962: 24 and passim). Concepts can become "frozen" in at least two ways. First, once established, especially when operationalized, concepts resist change against time and changing context. Second, given the greater importance of prose in the social sciences, there is a strong tendency when adopting a consensual concept to treat it as a unitary phenomenon, or, to put it another way, a strong tendency to impose a false unidimensionality on the concept.

A perfect case study in the conservatism of operationalizing (or any other consensus around a concept) is the liberal/conservative ideological continuum. In 1957, Anthony Downs based a substantial portion of his "economic theory of democracy" on the premise

that every voter's preferences are *single-peaked* and slope downward *monotonically* on either side of the peak … For example, if a voter likes position 35 best, we can immediately deduce that he prefers 30 to 25 and 40 to 45 (Downs 1957: 115–116; emphasis added).

Downs' definition of liberal/conservative at that time was the conventional, consensual one: on the liberal side, pro-government and pro-social change; on the conservative side, less of both. Move ahead 40 years and the definition remains the same, operationalized the same way in the polling and roll call data available. There was no reflection on whether time and circumstance had altered those meanings. More importantly, there was no discussion whatsoever as to the possibility that liberalism and conservatism are not opposite sides of a single continuum but are *two entirely different dimensions of ideology* (Lowi 1996: 218–232). One very good example of 40 years after Downs is David Brady, an outstanding behavioral scientist and rational choice "moderate". Brady's entire analysis in *Revolving Gridlock*, which is in the mainstream of rational choice, rests upon the "theoretical foundations" of the unidimensional spatial model of Downs' 1957 model (Brady and Volden 1998: 16–18 and 74–78).

Pluralism is another case in point. With everything written about it or drawn from it, and despite the yards of criticism and praise of pluralism as a solution to governance, we tend to get multiples of discrete narrative in which pluralism is the key word, and then we allow it to travel through its many cultural and temporal contexts by use of adjectives. With all the "varieties of pluralist experience" (to take a phrase from William James) we keep pluralism as a unitary concept (like religion) by adding adjectives. But the varieties of experience continue to remain apart, isolated in empirical splendor, with little if any logical connection between one pluralist experience and another – except the "contrast and compare" treatment we so often pose in Ph.D. exam questions.

Using a "qualitative methodology" developed in collaboration with Professor Mauro Calise, I hope to bring more useful theory to pluralism by unpacking this dense and overloaded concept. This is the essence of analysis, to break a concept into its parts, examine the parts, and put them back together in a more logical ordering. And this is virtually a definition of pre-theory (Calise and Lowi 2000: 285; Calise and Lowi 2003: 27–40.)[1]

As explained in the book's introduction, the method is in the matrix that will be presented below. It is based on the following understandings:

1. Concepts embody experience. Concepts, says Merton, "constitute the definitions (or prescriptions) of what is to be observed ..." (Merton 1957: 89).

2. As a consequence, concepts can become overloaded with "conceptual stretching", through adjectives and through discrete narratives loosely joined to the concept. The uncontrolled connotations, tantamount to ambiguity, rob the concept of value (Collier 1993: 845–855).

3. To preserve concept integrity, concepts must be defined by following the lexicological rule that a good definition must specify what the word is and also what it is *not*, i.e., each concept must have specified boundaries.

4. Concepts – especially the rich concepts that comprise the vocabulary of any science – must be defined by other concepts that limit and guide the applicability and the referents of the concept in question.

5. Concepts are typically used in association with one or more other concepts. Again with Merton, "when concepts are interrelated in the form of

---

1   I put "qualitative methodology" in quotes because I am not yet convinced that this has matured beyond the stage of oxymoron. I continue to think that what we are doing is more a case of good etiquette rather than established methodology that one can teach in terms of techniques to be acquired and applied.

a scheme ... a theory begins to emerge" (Merton 1957: 89). Reaching further back, to the Greeks, in particular Plato's dialogues, concepts tend to present themselves in "philosophical pairs", with one and its opposite, or one and its distance from another, as on a continuum (Schiappa 2003: 36–37).

6. Since the definitions of concepts are other concepts associated in pairs – as dialogue or dialectic – concepts defined this way can be "cross tabulated" or, with Merton, "codified", to establish and maintain logical relationships to all other concepts in the relevant universe of discourse (Merton 1957: 12–13 and 100–101). The standard method of definition is lexicographical – a dictionary definition. Even the *Oxford English Dictionary* is a linear definition, providing the essential meaning or meanings, with usages that provide history and context. Ours is 'hypertextual', placing the concept in a pattern of logical relations among concepts in a matrix. The concept in question (from here on, *entry* or *keyword*) is located between one set of pairs (a dichotomy) which is *cross-tabulated* with another pair. These are treated as axes whose cross-tabulation produces four "property spaces". And the box is then closed, with each choice of concept reducing the *degrees of freedom* of choice of the concepts selected as necessary to complete the matrix. It is a closed logical system in which a change in any concept has a bumping effect on all the others. (Such a change is not dysfunctional. It is the source of serendipity.)

The complete matrix must then be rendered into a prose, narrative definition in which all the concepts in the matrix are employed. Even a rough and partial rendering of such a definition comprised of 12 other paired concepts can be offered in itself as an operational definition of pre-theory. The matrix with its prose rendering is not a theory about some aspect of reality. The matrix may be considered a paradigm if we take the definition as "a set of propositions or meta-theoretic hypotheses aiming less at social reality than at the language used to study this social reality" (Boudon 1989: 410). Once again relying on Merton, "paradigms, by their very arrangement, suggest the systematic cross-tabulation of presumably significant concepts ... They promote analysis rather than concrete description ... [and] the codification of methods of qualitative analysis in a manner approximating the logical, if not empirical, rigor of quantitative analysis" (Merton 1957: 15 and passim).

II. The Pluralism Matrix

A Standard Treatment

Pluralism as a concept came into common usage in the early 20th century. The main source of the idea could be contributed to William James. He applied his pragmatist, "radically empiricist" philosophical views toward developing a many-dimensional position opposed to "monism", defined by him as a system of thought with only "one ultimate principle" (Ellis 2001). Other important sources were the German Otto von Gierke and the Briton Ernest Barker. Gierke's contribution was his 1880 writings that weakened "monism" with his discovery that the political theories of the Middle Ages made considerable use of the ideas "of a cooperative associational commonwealth" and "of representation … the exercise of the rights belonging to a community by a representative assembly" (Friedrich 1932: XXXV; Friedrich 1968: 269). Barker's was his 1914 formulation of the term "polyarchy" in appreciation of federalism and of Montesquieu's conception of the "mixed regime".

All this was brought together by Harold Laski, a student of Barker, who "politicized" pluralism during the 1920s, as part of a critique of the "monistic state" and the offering of an alternative. He stressed the importance (empirical and normative) of alternative forms of human association, including religious associations (from the more conservative viewpoint) and (from the left) the worker associations and trade unions or in guild and syndical associations. As did Tocqueville and many other foreign observers who came to criticize and stayed to marvel, Laski appreciated American pluralism for its "diversity, variety, localism, volunteerism" and "the variety of its group life, and the wide distribution of its sovereign powers" (Kramnick and Sheerman 1993: 103). Although his embrace of pluralism, which built up during his six-year residence in Boston, stayed with him throughout his professional life, Laski remained syndicalist and socialist in his native England – in fact was leader of the left wing of the British Labour Party (Kramnick and Sheerman 1993: 103–105). If there was ever to be a fusion of the two Laskis, it would be in a combination of pluralism and Marxism, governed by a congress of functional representation. Rainer Eisfeld treats this more thoroughly in his chapter.

The most important contribution to the Americanization of pluralism was that of Arthur F. Bentley (1908) in his seminal work *The Governmental Process*. Bentley elevated "the group" as the unit of analysis that was required for a systematic, objective, scientific study of politics and government. "The state", with its "sovereignty" and other "soul stuff", was considered a useless abstraction. Government, not the state, was the focus, and government in a stateless America exists as a process driven by the "pure activity" of what came to be called "pressure groups" or, more sanitized, "interest groups".

Though Bentley did not explicitly refer to himself or his approach as "plural-ist", he has to be considered the father of political pluralism in America (Seidelman 1985: 67–93). Bentley's conception is more in keeping with Madison's (1787) theory in *The Federalist No. 10*. In this theory, "faction" is an inherent product of freedom, except that for Madison these factions (or interest groups) were, again by nature, antagonistic to the public interest and had to be "regulated" (Madison's own word) by a constitution that fostered such a plurality of groups that their constant competition would reduce if not neutralize their influence, thus freeing the legislature to make more enlight-ened laws (Dahl 1956; Truman 1951).

Pluralism exists in the identities people develop out of the places, posi-tions and cleavages they occupy. Pluralism *is* civil society wherever the sepa-rate identities are allowed to develop and express themselves. Political pluralism exists as long as freedom to "petition the government" is tolerated. And competition between and among petitioners improves the probability of competition between and among elites, with such hypothesized consequences as restraint of power, decentralization of power, and transparency of govern-ment, with enhanced information and accountability. These hypotheses have been confirmed at least as measured by the rich fund of empirical research on the governmental process over the century of the existence of American po-litical science. In fact, it is too rich. The concept, with all its trappings, needs unpacking. This can best be done 'hypertextually' by defining the concept (entry) within the family of its closest conceptual relations, tying these to-gether in a closed logical matrix:

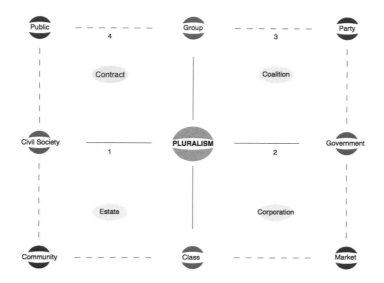

The Core of the Matrix: The Axes

The pairs of concepts chosen for the two axes are, in our judgment, the "concepts without which". We could in fact go a long way toward a satisfactory narrative definition of pluralism without the help of any other concepts. However, although they could guide the narrative, they would not take us far beyond the narrative.

The vertical axis comprehends the dimension of cleavage in society and the texture of associations within cleavages. Group-to-class, class-to-group is a continuum but with deep breaks in continuity, where differences of degree amount to differences of principle. Group is the concept most appropriate for associations constituted by the highest degree of "rational choice"; that is, group affiliations are primarily in terms of shared values and objectives. Class refers to associations constituted by the highest degree of "determined choice"; that is, affiliations arise primarily out of the place of individuals in relation to the market or other pre-existing or inherited social or cultural hierarchies. Class means classification, within which individuals take on substantive perspectives more probably ascribed and inherited than chosen. Marxism was correct in its assertion that a preponderance of attitudes and ideologies are socially or economically determined. But to insist that all are determined by ascribed class is to deny the possibility of a Marx. Intellectual life in class or caste ends the moment people begin to associate around a shared complaint or hope. A trade union is no longer an assemblage of proletariat. It has moved along the continuum from class to group – to interest group.

The horizontal axis comprehends the dimension of orientation or objective – to *be* the state or to influence the state. Laski's English syndicalism was the radical idea of displacing the state with functional self-government in a "classless society". Ernest Barker's observations made during the darkest moments of democracy in the 1930s emphasize not only the substantive texture of groups but the extremes of radicalism that are produced by the forming of groups out of classes or castes and in the expansion of such groups back toward incorporation of the entire class from which they sprang – through broadening substantive interests into ideologies of antagonism toward the state or the civil society. And he speaks of totalitarian groups that arise out of castes or ethnic subdivisions that attempt to provide for all the needs of its members as small states-within-the state, and thence into sponsorship by an ultimate "wedding" to the state (Barker 1958: 155–167).

The Peripherals

The peripheral concepts at the corners are obviously an attempt to "close off" the axes. Here already is where we begin to appreciate how each new concept reduces the "degrees of freedom" for the next and the next concept, until the last concept is virtually imposed.

The choice for the peripheral concepts must be to the fullest extent possible derived from or at least inspired by the three points created by the entry and two of the polar points of the axes. There is of course a great deal of pure intuition in these choices – or better, inspiration – because the three concepts already present sends us back to the literature of social science. But still, our imagination is restricted by the need to provide the fourth corner in a way that is logically and substantively comfortable with the other three points. We chose as our criterion "arena", the field of play. Thus, to begin, if "group" and "government" are the two definers of the pluralism of the upper right quadrant, it is pointing toward the "classic" American version of pluralism, the *party* arena. By the same criterion, the best available choice for the lower right peripheral was *market*, because it, like party, is in a dynamic arena in which very large numbers of preferences are ordered. This arena is as pluralistic as the American "factions" Madison defined in *The Federalist No. 10*.

The two peripherals on the right – party and market – are fields of play that can be characterized as "political pluralism". Market should not appear anomalous here, because, at least for the past three or more centuries, it has been a "political economy" dependent upon the state for protection of property and maintenance of the rules of exchange. The two peripherals on the left are fields of play that can be characterized as "social pluralism". The upper left, public, may at first seem anomalous but was selected to refer to life outside the household (which was once the literal Greek meaning of *economy*). We would have chosen society as the arena opposite "community" – following the well-known continuum in sociology, *Gemeinschaft-Gesellschaft* – but society seemed a bit too diffuse for present purposes.

The Property Spaces

At this point we are all the more constrained by our previous choices. Our choice to fill the spaces delineated by the four points that create each space was guided by the single criterion of what in our judgment was the most prominent institutional arrangement for the respected dynamics and textures of the various pluralisms. Politics in government-centered pluralisms is coalitional. In European parliamentary systems, the coalition is usually comprised of relations *between* parties or representatives of parties in the governing coalition. In an American/presidential system, coalitions are comprised of groups *within* the parties, especially the governing party. The lower right, corporation, is the ultimate equilibrium of market dynamics. It is the coming together of wealth, exchange, contract in the form of a fictive person, created out of recognition by the state – in a charter – enabling the corporation to act as a unit, to hold property, make contracts, to sue and be sued and to die as a person without holding any of the owners (stockholders) responsible beyond their shares in the corporation. The lower left, estate denotes an institutionalism of determined preferences, prescribed hierarchies and ascribed places within hierarchies. The upper left, contract, could be replaced by participation, which for many is the modern definition of civil society. But contract – or contractualism as a social dynamic, a process – adds an institutional or equilibrium dimension, as implied by the notion of voluntary association, which is to agree to cooperate or to agree on what to disagree about. This is Rousseau's "social contract", the creation of a General Will that makes the state part of non-coercive civil society rather than a separate, Weberian monopolist of legal coercion. See also Burke's critique of the contractual society in the next section.

III. Pluralisms: A Rendering of the Matrix

Type 1: Feudal Pluralism

The lower left quadrant, bounded by civil society, community and class, comes first because it is a *pre-state pluralism*, both in temporal and conceptual terms – in a word, feudalism. Feudalism was its own kind of pluralism. It was a pluralism composed of community – or communal – life, castes, consociations, status hierarchies and incipient states-within-the nation or society (or city-states-within-the-nation or society). But feudalism – or practices and textures prominent in feudalism – did not end with the consolidation of nation-states. Feudalism was in many respects the bridge between antiquity and "modern" society and politics; and a great deal of this quadrant is alive today in varying degrees in different parts of the world.

During the heyday of feudalism, sovereignty and monism were only emerging. Laski was among many to observe that "the state is only one of many forms of human association" (Ellis 2001). Feudal societies were composed largely of communal, spontaneous small units or "estates" built on ascription. This element of association remained even as the spreading interaction between and among communities produced larger social units as the countryside was pacified and markets began to spring up at or near every intersection of two "highways".

This is captured in an important pair of concepts (a continuum, developed by Ferdinand Toennies, Georg Simmel and others in the distinction between *Gemeinschaft* and *Gesellschaft*): primary versus secondary association or, as described by Merton, local versus cosmopolitan (Merton 1957: 317ff and

393). That implies modernization, but modernization did not come with the abruptness and totality that revolution implies.

Expansion of feudal society from a collection of communities, castes and guilds toward a *people*, not yet a *public*, was accomplished to a great extent by *patronage*. Patronage is one of the most important legacies of feudalism. Sweeping away the vulgarized usage of today – as the distribution of public jobs (in a "spoils system") by the victorious political party – patronage is a distinct, fundamental method of human association. It was "a permanent structural characteristic of all early European material high culture ..." (Gundersheimer 1981: 3). Patronage can be defined simply as a method of distributing the surplus resources of a "patron" on an individualized basis to one or more "clients". This is done as payment for services, as a reward for desired activities, as a means of cooption or purchase of loyalties, or to strengthen legitimacy, etc., in order to sustain organized life in family, community, clan, guild, class, and other subunits in a highly pluralized, unintegrated nation or society.

Edmund Burke (1790), in his defense of traditional society – which was late feudalism in England – concentrated his most passionate (and probably most famous) attack on the modern, rationally constituted "contractual" society. Anticipating Henry Maine by 70 years, in Maine's brilliant summation of modernization as the passage "from status to contract" (Maine 1861), Burke attacked the entire principle of contract as an individualist principle that undermines true membership in communities and therefore destroys "access to all the stores of culture ... that makes the difference between savagery and civilization":

Society is indeed a contract ... but the state ought not to be considered as nothing better than a partnership agreement in a trade of pepper and coffee, calico or tobacco, ... to be dissolved by the fancy of the parties. It is to be looked on with other reverence ... As the ends of such a partnership cannot be obtained in many generations, it becomes a partnership not only between those who are living, but between those who are living, those who are dead, and those who are to be born. Each contract of each particular state is but a clause in the great primeval contract of eternal society, linking the lower with the higher natures ... all physical and moral natures, each in their appointed place (Burke 1999: 192–193; Sabine 1950: 615).

Burke was a conservative; in fact his classic work, cited here, earned him credit as the founding father of conservatism. But he was also a defender of the late feudal system of Great Britain, with its monarchy, its free-standing communities and its hierarchy of aristocracy, clergy, gentility and serfdom. Burke drew no clear distinction between society and state, first because the English state was neither prosperous nor strong in the 18th century and, more importantly, because in Burke's view people are governed by, and society is held together by, a combination of religion and patronage. As monistic states displaced loose and pluralist feudal societies, a feudal or post-feudal nation held together by religion and patronage, in a world of nations preying on each other, would be a most fragile political entity. And its most dangerous threat would come from nation-states that had fostered the march "from status to contract". It was the late 18th century version of "globalization" that inspired Adam Smith to write his great treatise against mercantilism – the policy of feudal and post-feudal nations to protect their old societies from the incursions of young capitalism. The same holds true today. The most violent reactions to expanding trade and capitalist rationality have been in 20th century feudal and post-feudal holdovers: rich in resources held together by the estate of religiously enforced castes, by patronage drawn from natural resource surpluses, and by dictatorship where a state of patronage proved insufficient.

Type 2: Market-Driven Pluralism

Even if market-driven pluralism seems to be a step in historical sequence from Type 1, this hypothesis should be pursued with care. Although Mosca characterized the difference between these two systems as "feudal versus bureaucratic", he added the caveat, that "a society [can] pass back and forth between feudalism and bureaucracy any number of times" (Mosca 1939: 81). The "feudal state" is "that type of political organization in which all the executive functions of society ... are exercised simultaneously by the same individuals, while at the same time the state is made up of small aggregates, each of which possesses all of the organs that are required for self sufficiency" (Mosca 1939: 83). (Note the extreme pluralism of that observation.)

The matrix indicates, however, that there are two developments. First, we have entered the realm of the state and state-centered politics – a tendency toward monism, with the state as the center of discourse. Second, there is movement along the community-to-market continuum. This is a quadrant of *faction*, as Madison put it so well in *The Federalist No. 10*: Faction is a spontaneous association "sewn in the nature of man" arising out of "a zeal for different opinions", the most important (i.e., dangerous) sources of faction being "the various and unequal distribution of property".

Tocqueville was also struck by the American preference for voluntary association, contrasting the result with associations in Europe, which "consider themselves ... as the legislative and executive council of the people ... naturally led to adopt an organization which is not civic and peaceable, but partakes of the habit and maxims of military life" (Tocqueville 1959: 54).

But as it turned out, Europe was just one step ahead, with the tendency of groups to incorporate, i.e., to make themselves permanent. Adam Smith was on the trail of something like this in his observation that "people of the same trade seldom meet together, even for merriment and diversion, but the conversation ends in a conspiracy against the public" (Smith 1981: I:145). He also paid special attention to the formation of Guilds and other types of corporations, with or without the sponsorship of the crown or a local government (Smith 1981: I:141). What Smith and Tocqueville were witnessing was, to be mundane, a "political process" in which associations – mainly in trade but also in civic and cultural matters – were seeking public patronage, an old form of government confronting not merely estates, castes and upper class dependencies. This is a feudal carry-over that will remain throughout modernization. The corporate form is the essential core of pluralism in the market-driven society. We in political science tend to view these groups too narrowly as "interest groups" organized to influence public policy. That is true and important, but quite incomplete, because the very existence of these corporate (or incorporated) groupings is political.

In the U.S., with its federalism and its weak and narrow national government, the organization of interests went where the power was lodged – in the politics at state and at local governments. Because most moral issues requiring regulation were "reserved" to the states, groups other than normal economic interests abounded; and they operated the same way with the same strategies as economic groups. But at all levels of government in the U.S., the pluralism was the genuine article: a true multiplicity of organized interests, relatively autonomous, competing with each other for political influence and, to a large extent, as Madison had hoped: the very competition among this multiplicity of groups would contribute toward the neutralization or "regulation" of their power. The selfish nature of these independently organized factions made them by nature antagonistic to any concept of "the public interest". But suppressing them or isolating them from politics would not only be contrary to the First Amendment but would surely be a cure worse than the disease. Thus, the only remedy for all the mischievous consequences of pluralism was *more pluralism*: "Extend the sphere [of government] and you take in a greater variety of parties and interests; … and … it will be more difficult … to act in unison with each other" (Madison 1787: 83).

Countries with stronger national state institutions and a stronger tradition of state centeredness also became more politically pluralist as they liberalized and democratized. However, precisely because the statist tradition was so much stronger, their pluralism was much more corporatist – i.e., the state took a stronger interest in patronizing and, through that, regulating their pluralism. It is no accident that the first systematic use of the term "corporatism" or "corporativism" was Mussolini in his writings during his socialist phase of the post-World War I period; it was then elevated to central position in his *Doctrine of Fascism* in 1931 (Barker 1958: 341 and Chapter XII passim). In many respects, the socialists, the more radical communists, the anarchists and the fascists put more stress on corporatist groups than on party, even though the successful movements in Russia, Italy and Germany (in that order) ended up obliterating the autonomy of corporate groups by incorporating them into the totalitarian, governing party. This will return in Quadrant 4.

Type 3: Party-Driven Pluralism

Political pluralism in the U.S. sits astride quadrants 1, 2 and 3, not because the U.S. violates the logic of the scheme but because of its vastness, its federal system, and its movement over time. Thus, 19th century American politics moves across from quadrant 1 to 2. But even as Tocqueville was making his observation in the 1830s American pluralism was changing. There were more groups of the corporate type. Second, the concentration of capital contributed to cleavages across the society along class lines, adding to factional pluralism a struggle between market-driven corporate groups and class-based associations that came to be called social movements. Third, American political parties were establishing their bases outside the legislatures (Congress and the state legislature), grounded in electoral districts and institutionalizing themselves as a system of two competing parties in almost every state and county in the U.S. American pluralism thus enters Quadrant 3.

Maurice Duverger quite correctly classifies these American parties as "bourgeois parties", like the French Radical Party of that epoch, "which recruits no members", and remains a "cadre" party, "a party [which] is not a community but a collection of communities ..." (Duverger 1951: 17 ff, 62 ff). These are to be contrasted with socialist and other "branch" parties, where recruiting of members is a fundamental activity; and "what the mass party secures by numbers, the cadre party achieves by selection" (Duverger 1951: 63–64). In many American local and state situations, these bourgeois cadre parties were so well organized and deeply rooted in the community that they literally internalized pluralism – much the way European mass-oriented "branch" parties had succeeded in doing. This was the era of the "machine" in the United States, with its "bosses" who were deeply communally tied to local life, customs and interests. The political power of these machines and many other parties came from their ability to mobilize and exploit local groups and classes (economic, ethnic and religious) for electoral purposes. They held such a monopoly of access to government that all groups, including the wealthiest of corporate groups, had to make their peace with the machine. One of the "latent functions" of these parties was to act as a buffer between organized interests and government, providing a relatively peaceful channel of potential influence for class politics to be played by the lower agricultural and laboring classes.[2] This was in effect the golden age of political parties in

---

2   See Robert Merton for the distinction between "latent functions" and "manifest functions" of social and political activities. Chapters 1 and 2, especially his use of the political machine as a case study, pp. 72–82.

the United States. It was indeed "party democracy". They ran elections and performed as intermediaries or buffers between civil society and government. And institutionally, their absorption of interest groups converted the parties into *coalitional parties*. "Coalition" is a special form of relation in which competing units agree to coordinate action on a limited number of objectives; or, as the *Oxford English Dictionary* puts it, coalition is "an alliance for combined action of distinct parties, persons, or states, without permanent incorporation into one body". This made American parties a bit more like European parties, although coalitions of groups were internalized within the *parties* in the United States, whereas in Europe, coalitions tended to be within *government*, combining two or more parties into a working majority, or, as the parliamentary language put it, "to form a government". Thus, from a starting point opposite Europe, American parties played a role similar to European parties by providing a channel of influence for class politics. One of the great moments in American history was the sudden inclusion of agriculturalists *as a class* into the Democratic party with a speech by presidential candidate William Jennings Bryan, his "cross of gold" speech committing the Democratic party to a policy of some degree of redistribution of wealth. That new coalition expanding beyond the southern Democratic party base remained influential long enough to play a major role in the formation of progressive reform legislation of 1910–1914, nationwide and in the states.

But classic party government was short-lived in the U.S. Applying Dahl's definition of political modernization, there was a movement from "cumulative inequalities" toward "dispersed inequalities" (Dahl 1961: 85–86; Huntington 1968: 33). The "interest group" was beginning to lead a life all its own. Here is a case in which academic observers were ahead of the historical curve. What appeared to be the height of party government turned out to be its apogee – as one group after another abandoned the party monopoly of access to government, continuing to play coalition politics but increasingly dealing directly with government independent of mediation or filtration by parties. Arthur F. Bentley anticipated this in his 1908 book with what was later to be called "the group theory of politics", but it had to wait 45 years to be embraced (Bentley 1908; Truman 1951). Class-based movements, voluntary associations, corporate groups and legally incorporated groups all become what can best be called "rational choice pluralism".

Parties continued to play a role of mediator but rational choice interest groups were seeking bargaining relationships directly with governments, in particular the administrative agencies of government. Agriculture moved early from an all-agriculture class movement to a multiplicity of "commodity groups" and sectional "agri-business" groups. Labor as a class (in the U.S. and elsewhere) became a multiplicity of trade union organizations. George Bernard Shaw picked up on this with the acerbic observation that "trade unions are the capitalism of the proletariat" (Bell 1960: 208). Shaw had English and European unions in mind but to a certain extent it applies everywhere, but most accurately in the U.S. – the world center of development from ascribed associations to rational choice interest groups.

Type 4: Corporate Pluralism

A useful linkage to Type 4 is Lindblom's 1977 book whose thesis did not have the impact on political science or public discourse that it should have, possibly because it was unselfconsciously neo-Marxian and insufficiently normative:

We begin this analysis by exploring ... the political role of businessmen in all private en-terprise market-oriented societies. This role ... is not ... merely an interest-group role ... Because public functions in the market system rest in the hands of businessmen ... gov-ernment officials cannot be indifferent ... A major function of government, therefore, is to see to it that businessmen perform their tasks (Lindblom 1977: 170 and 172–173).

In this lies what Lindblom rightly calls "the privileged position of business" (the title of Chapter 3). He continues:

In the eyes of government officials, therefore, businessmen do not appear simply as the representatives of a special interest, as representatives of interest groups do. They appear as functionaries performing functions that government officials regard as indispensable ... Any government official who understands ... the responsibilities that market-oriented sys-tems throw on business will therefore grant them a privileged position. He does not have to be bribed, duped or pressured ... Collaboration and deference between the two are at the heart of politics in such system ... (Lindblom 1977: 75)

Lindblom strengthens the linkage to Type 4 with a profoundly important point he merely drops in along with some illustrations of the extent of, but with no reflection on, its significance: "... We shall see below that governments sometimes offer to share their formal authority with corporate officials as a benefit offered to induce business performance" (op. cit.: 174). And a few pages later (op. cit.: 185–188) Lindblom gives several relevant illustrations, from grants of eminent domain power to private utility corporations, to "out-sourcing" military projects of both a civil and strategic nature, to business councils in agriculture programs, and with references to still more extensive "business authority in government" in France, the UK and Germany. Bear in mind that this was written a good ten years before the European Union had become an operative institution with extensive penetration of private corpora-tions into EU decisions in Brussels.

The most appropriate concept for characterizing Quadrant 4 is of course *corporatism. Ism* as a suffix has several meanings, but prominent among them is its use as a class-name for a doctrine, belief or theory. As doctrine and the-ory, corporatism (or corporativism) is in effect a plan for a state organized into corporations representing employers and employees – and thence the nation. To move on beyond Lindblom, corporatism is in effect the institution-alization and legitimation of the "privileged position of business". This takes pluralism well beyond the group competition and "bargaining among elites" and party-group coalitions of Type 3. Business interests still operate through interest groups, lobbying and more recently trying to influence elections di-rectly through Political Action Committees in the U.S. and more informally elsewhere. However, in the sharing of public authority, each corporation op-erates as its own interest group, with influence *in* government rather than in-fluence *on* government.

The best comprehensive, comparative survey of the role of corporations with "privileged positions" sharing public authority is that of Janine Wedel. Wedel coined her own term, "flex organization" to capture the "movement toward privatization" in the 1980s and 1990s, especially following the Soviet collapse, with "non-state actors [to] ... fulfill functions once reserved for the state". And she stresses "the inclination to blur 'state' and 'private' spheres". In various forms and under various names, these flex organizations now enjoy global acceptance – "from Washington to Warsaw to Wellington" (Wedel 2004).

However, although Wedel delves into the risks involved with the blurring of public and private roles and offers a number of instructive cases waving the warning flag against conflicts of interest, lack of transparency, poor ac-countability and weakening of state authority (especially in former socialist regimes), she fails to tie these recent developments into the traditional experi-ence with corporatism and its special association with previous authoritarian regimes associated with fascism. And it is on this point a conclusion can be drawn, with both empirical and normative characterization of Type 4.

The corporate form is surely the feature of society that governments pre-fer to deal with. The corporate structure is stable and durable. It is a perma-nent collectivity – in fact it is an eternal person. It is above its individual members but is accountable through the fiduciary relation to the members (stockholders). The corporation is compatible with government bureaucracy because of its own bureaucratic structure and the tendency of all bureaucrats to think alike. Mannheim in his sociology of knowledge has characterized all bureaucratic thought "as conservatism". Bureaucratic conservatism is "the tendency to turn all problems of politics into problems of administration". Reality is a "smoothly functioning order", in which the unpredictable is irra-tional, and irrational factors are treated as "routine matters of state" (Mann-heim 1929 and 1936: 118–119). And the corporation is relatively easy to adjust to because of the public character of corporatism, due to the state grant of privilege in the corporate charter. Corporations have thus blurred the public-private distinction even as their apologists stress the virtues of "the private sector" and how modern government is menacing capitalism by violat-ing the sanctity of the private sector.

Lindblom does not go far enough with the "privileged position of business", because in his hands it implies independent corporations that are in effect on the government payroll to ensure the performance of business. That is one variant, still in Quadrant 3 or tending toward Quadrant 4. But corporatism goes much further. Corporatism is a tendency in all Quadrants, but mature corporatism is the most highly sought after form of pluralism in countries with weak regimes or failed regimes whose governments seek to revive or survive by loaning sovereignty in return for support and legitimacy. Corporatist pluralism (for corporations and unions) was highly sought-after in the 1920s and 1930s by most developed countries in Asia, Europe and in the U.S., beginning with Herbert Hoover.

As Secretary of Commerce for eight years under his two Republican presidential predecessors, Hoover wrote copiously and pursued in practice the theory that "volunteer associations" would solve the problem of government power, and he used his powers as Secretary of Commerce to sponsor the formation of important trade associations, comprised of their constituent corporations. When Franklin Delano Roosevelt adopted the same approach to the economic crisis, ex-President Hoover called Roosevelt's program fascism, but this is only because Roosevelt was more bold in using Hoover's own principles. Corporatism was the dominant feature of his effort to revive industry (National Recovery Act), agriculture (Agricultural Adjustment Act), and finance (Securities and Exchange Commission and the Federal Reserve System's expansion) (Lowi 1967 and 1979; Brand 1988).

The corporatist pattern was revived in many recovering states after World War II, from France and Italy to Japan; and elements, albeit less pronounced, were present in England and the U.S. (Einaudi, Byé, and Rossi 1955). Post-Soviet weak states, especially Russia, abound in corporatism. Corporatism is receiving a still more positive spin in the publications generated by the emergence, expansion and success of the European Community into the European Union. "Interest group" and "pressure group" have been sanitized as "non-governmental groups", known affectionately as NGOs. There are still other state-private hybrids that have come into prominence, such as QUANGOs (quasi-nongovernmental organizations) and GONGOs (government-organized NGOs) (Wedel 2001; Wedel 2004). All of these are getting official recognition and they are taking on many kinds of essentially governmental functions. Typical words associated with the legitimizing of these corporatist practices are: partnerships, outsourcing, privatization, devolution, and "democratic corporatism" (Schmitter 1974; Katzenstein 1985, Chapters 1 and 3; Lijphart 1999; Thelen 1991; Wedel 2001).

What has been neglected in virtually all of these writings is the danger inherent in Type 4 pluralism. And polyarchy is no cleansing agent. Although Type 4 Corporate pluralism is a great distance from its feudal ancestors of Quadrant 1 – with its pluralism of estates, castes and communal associations

– the DNA would demonstrate an ancestral relationship. We need hardly repeat the earlier caveat that the developmental relation among quadrants is not unidirectional. The modern corporatist pluralism of Quadrant 4 is "functional feudalism", with satrapies whose share of participation in state power is close to ownership, sanitized as partnership and privatization, and legitimized as elite competition resembling the "dispersed inequalities" of the market-driven and party driven pluralism of Quadrants 2 and 3.

The U.S. can be considered a case of leapfrogging Quadrant 3 in response to the Great Depression, going deep into Quadrant 4 for three decades before becoming something more of a state-centered and party-centered pluralism of Quadrant 3, in what came to be called a welfare state. Unions as interests groups were a vital part of that pluralism, but many union leaders feared as early as the 1930s that labor as a movement would lose its strength if employment security were provided by government rather than by the union-organized workplaces. In other words, "labor rights" would come from the labor-management "syndicate".

This was the thrust of the demand for collective bargaining and the union shop, a divide-and-conquer strategy in which the union would be the guardian and the employer would be the provider of rights. Henry Ford anticipated this before the Depression with his Five Dollar Day (well above the prevailing wage) as part of a paternalistic view of labor. And in the fateful 1941 year for labor, he cemented relations with his main adversary, the United Auto Workers, by recognizing UAW as the bargaining agent and by accepting not only a union shop but virtually a closed shop (with union pre-clearance of employees). Companies in the other basic industries – mining and steel in particular – followed suit. This was topped later by an initiative in 1948 by General Motors with an offer to "privatize" economic security with a Cost of Living Adjustment (COLA) pegged to the official cost of living index. The radical UAW leader Walter Reuther embraced the offer, calling it a "blue plate special". By the early 1960s, the COLA principle had been implanted in more than 50 percent of all major union contracts (Lichtenstein 2002: 122–125; Dulles and Dubofsky 1993: 313–318).[3]

All this points to a general tendency of large corporations to seek employee stability by creating a syndicalist satrapy, making itself a corporate "company town". This is the ultimate "Fordism", to gain efficiency by systematizing and unitizing work (the ultimate is the character of Charlie Chaplan's *Modern Times*) but then humanizing the relationship by incorporating as many elements of communal life as is possible. The best available image is the corporate company town, a chartered mini-state-within-the-state, providing income, income security and what has come to be called social

---

3   For a quite recent indication of the tendency of union leaders to favor a corporatist
    solution, see Robert Fitch, "Big Labor's Secret: Why Self-Interested Unions Are Blocking
    Health Care Reform", *New York Times*, December 28, 2005, p. A19.

capital. As long as employees remain in good standing, they are, in effect, citizens of their company, having their rights as citizens of the company, enjoying more of their rights as citizens of the company than the more remote state.

Quadrant 4 demonstrates the logic of this, not necessarily the inevitability. The union shop and the management/oversight of the contract were the beginning of the decline of the so-called labor movement, ending in what Lichtenstein has called "the private welfare state" (Lichtenstein 2002: 125 passim). This is the corporatist synthesis: a competition between Quadrant 3 – the public welfare state that universalizes social rights with a wedge between employment and employer – and Quadrant 4 corporatism, whose anthem could be the 1955 song of the great country and western singer, Tennessee Ernie Ford: "So tell St. Peter that I can't go, 'cause I owe my soul to the comp'ny sto'."[4]

---

4   My thanks to Shari Jacobson for explaining that the music was Ford's and the words were by Merle Travis.

Rainer Eisfeld

Pluralism and Democratic Governance:
A Century of Changing Research Frameworks

I. A Pluralist Perspective on Capitalist Democracy: Empirical Diagnoses, Normative Visions, Legitimating Ideologies

Theorizing about the presumed pluralist structure of Western capitalist societies and about the access pluralist players have in fact, and should have, to the
setting of public agendas commenced in earnest a century ago. Emerging in
the early 20th century when it was finally recognized that the small, non-
industrial community envisaged by "classical" political theory had, for most
practical purposes, disappeared, the original variety of pluralism was constructed as a *critical* political theory (cf. Gettell 1924: 470), providing an
approach both descriptive and prescriptive.

Even before World War I, business corporations and industrial combines
– the first multinationals among them – had risen to prominence, underscor-
ing the unequal distribution of power between labor and capital. However, if
continuing entrepreneurial hegemony seemed assured, a century had also
passed since Adam Smith's grim dictum that the laboring poor were destined,
by "the progress of the division of labor", to remain "as stupid and ignorant as
it is possible for a human creature to become" (Smith 1776: 366). After bitter
struggles, a labor movement had emerged. Unions had been organized, and in
most industrialized countries the right to strike had been won.

Concurrently, the 19th century's rigid class structure was already dissolv-
ing. The working class was segmenting into numerous blue- and white-collar
strata – groups, in fact – differentiated by vocation and attitude, by income
and education and, again, by grossly unequal influence and control both economically and politically.

The intellectual climate seemed to be ready for a "new" political concept,
analytical no less than normative, reformulating the notions of freedom and
democracy in a determined attempt at attaining the "good society" in the context provided by organized capitalism and the large nation state. The answer
was a theory of associations, of positive, interventionist government and of a
more participatory political system, with industrial democracy as a comple-
ment of political democracy. In 1915, the British Labor Party intellectual
Harold J. Laski gave the name "pluralism" to the new approach, borrowing

the term from the pragmatist philosophy of William James who had used it to describe the character of a "distributive" reality (in contrast to monist ideas, particularly Hegel's, about a unified "bloc universe").

Less than half a century later, "pressure politics", the lobbying activities by which organized groups, now including labor, were seeking to influence parties, legislatures, governments and administrative bureaucracies, had become increasingly topical. At the same time, against the backdrop of the Cold War, the need was felt for a comprehensive theoretical perspective designed to explain and justify the political systems of the "free world", meaning the United States and post-World War II Western Europe. Stripped of most of its prescriptive – certainly its anticapitalist – implications, reduced to a "legitimating discourse" (Merelman 2003: 9) and in tune with "realistic" Schumpeterian theories of democratic elitism prevalent at the time (see, e.g., Held 2003: 200), the concept of pluralism (supplemented now, more often than not, by the prefix 'liberal' or 'neo-', in contrast to 'radical') seemed to serve the purpose perfectly.

Another five decades later, nation-states in North America, Western Europe and elsewhere are being affected by growing economic-financial globalization and permeation no less than by increasing ethnocultural pluralization and diversification, due to regional and global migratory movements. The pattern of societal cleavages and linkages is changing, the fragmentation of interests furthered, the role of the positive state is questioned, adherence to traditional institutional loyalties put in jeopardy. How, then, can we accept both economic globalization and the further pluralization of plural societies without, on the one hand, sacrificing electoral responsiveness and governmental accountability and, on the other, furthering a fundamentalization of group values that would, in Arthur Schlesinger's phrase, "disunite" society and polity?

Once again, the concept of pluralism may come to the rescue. Because the concept's endorsement of diversity is considered to include cultural multiplicity, a "revived pluralist perspective" now stands for "full and pluralist cultural inclusiveness" (McLennan 1995: 40) – for the assertion and public expression, the institutionalization even, of ethnocultural differences, provided that basic rights and principles of justice remain respected and protected. However, it is precisely the extent of differentiated treatment to be accorded to ethnic groups, in order to protect and develop their special cultural characteristics and practices, which has been the subject of continuing controversy. So far, this debate has achieved nothing which even remotely resembles conceptual clarity.

The specific problem illustrates a general point. Every variety of political pluralism so far put forward has been critically challenged: Early radical pluralism by liberal pluralism, with the challenge returned later for good measure; liberal pluralism, in addition, by neo-corporatism; cultural pluralism by a liberal individualism arguing in favor of impartiality. *Actually, there have never been full-fledged "theories" of pluralism, but rather empirical and normative research programs focusing on the means, constraints, and perspectives of societal participation in the shaping of public policies.* Frameworks for these programs have included the web of social organizations which has increasingly been referred to as civil society, the linkages of individuals, associations and governments (ranging from the internal government of associations to the pressures exerted by such organizations on each other and on state administrations), the building of legitimacy, consensus and cohesion on the basis of conflictual interests, the validity of the traditional division into private and public spheres (with ensuing limitations on the applicability of democratic principles), inequalities in the availability of political resources, finally the powers and the rights of majorities and minorities.

In the final analysis, successive pluralist research programs have amounted to nothing less than a persistent inquiry into the theory and practice of democracy under changing socio-economic and socio-cultural conditions.

II. Underpinning Political by Economic Democracy: Harold Laski and the Emergence of Radical Pluralism

As noted at the outset, the first two decades of the 20th century "revealed new problems of economic and political power for which the older democrats, whether liberals or socialists, had no ready solutions" (Beer 1975: IX). American philosophical pragmatism, developed by William James and insisting, as it did, on a "pluralistic" – rather than a monistic – interpretation of the cosmos, assumed "vital significance" for the slowly emerging "pluralistic theory of the state" (Laski 1921: 169; id. 1917: 23): None of reality's elements "includes everything or dominates everything ... The pluralistic world is thus more like a federal republic, than an empire or a kingdom ... However much may be collected, ... something else is self-governed ... and unreduced to unity" (James 1909: 208). Translated into political terms, such a "pluralistic universe" could be construed as a polity where groups, associated for "essential social ends" and "eliciting individual loyalties", evolved naturally, possessing inherent rights not conceded by the state (Coker 1924: 89, 93).

Harold Laski went even further. With "group competing against group", the state, as he would maintain in a 1915 lecture delivered at Columbia University, had to prove its superiority "by virtue of its moral program". Only in this way could it claim obedience from its citizens. And in a typical turn, which heralded the further development of his position, Laski added: "A state may in theory exist to secure the highest life for its members. But when we come to the analysis of the hard facts it becomes painfully apparent that the good actually maintained is that of a certain section, not the community as a whole. I should be prepared to argue, for instance, that in England before the war the ideal of the trade unions was a wider ideal than that which the state had attained" (Laski 1917: 15, 23).

The ideas of the Fabian Society, that intellectual circle of "respectable" socialists – established, among others, by Sidney and Beatrice Webb and George Bernard Shaw – which took part in the formation of the British Labour Party, considerably influenced Harold Laski's thinking. So did the argument of the guild socialists ("young rebels" in the Fabian ranks, building on French anarcho-syndicalism), particularly G. D. H. Cole, who held that associations sprang up in society according to the logic of functional differentiation and that self-government, consequently, was identical with functional representation on every social level (see Eisfeld 1996: 269/270, 272 ss.). That definitely included the workplace, the factory, the enterprise – in a nutshell, "control of production" by worker organizations –, since individuals (having, by steps, been enfranchised in the political sphere) had remained "enslaved" by industrial autocracy in the economic sector (Cole 1918: 40, 103 ss.).

Like Cole, Harold Laski remained convinced that "no political democracy (could) be real" without being underpinned by "an economic democracy" (Laski 1919: 38). Like Cole, too, he initially envisioned that the body politic should be "divide(d) upon the basis of functions", resulting in a dual legislature: a vocational Congress – after a transition period of joint industrial control by labor and capital – and a territorial Parliament. "Joint questions" would have to be solved by "joint adjustment" (Laski 1919b: 74, 87 ss.). Avoiding the term "conflict", Laski made no provision for any mechanism whose role went beyond mere "coordination". A certain "weakness on the constructive side" (Ellis 1923: 596) was apparent.

In his 1925 magnum opus entitled a *Grammar of Politics*, Laski retained two central contentions:

- "The structure of social organisation involves, not myself and the state, my groups and the state, but all these and their interrelationships ... The interest of the community is the total result of the whole pressure of social forces" (Laski 1925: 141, 261).

- "Exactly as the evolution of political authority has been concerned with the erection of limitations upon the exercise of power, so also with economic authority ... In a sense not less urgent than that in which Lincoln used it, no state can survive that is half-bond and half-free. The citizen ... must be given the power to share in the making of those decisions which affect him as a producer if he is ... to maximize his freedom" (ibid.: 112/113).

Repudiating the institutional project of the guild socialists whose difficulties he had come to consider "insurmountable" (ibid.: 72), Laski now focused on that distinction which would remain pivotal to conceptions of democratizing society: the distinction between ownership of the means of production and their control (ibid.: 112):

- "Just as the holder of government bonds has no control ... over government policy, so it is possible to prevent interference with the direction of an industrial enterprise by the loaners thereto of capital ... The present system of private property does not in the least involve the present technique of industrial direction."

It required the Great Depression of 1929 and the circumstances of the formation of the British National Government in 1931 for Laski to move more clearly in a Marxian direction without, however, as has been erroneously suggested, "rejecting" pluralism (Deane 1955: 153). Rather, by combining pluralism and Marxism, he proposed in 1937 to transcend the capitalist system, envisaging not violent action but, in a term Laski was to coin during World War II, a "revolution by consent" (Laski 1925: XII):

- "The purpose of pluralism merges into a larger purpose ... The object of the pluralist must be the classless society ... If the main ground of conflict is thus removed, it becomes possible to conceive of a social organization in which the truly federal nature of society receives institutional expression. And in such a social organization, authority can be pluralistic both in form and expression."

In modern terms, Laski's pluralism aimed at a more participatory democracy and an employee-controlled economy, diminishing the discretionary exercise and grossly unequal distribution of organizational – political and economic – power. *'Radical' pluralism, as it came to be called (Apter 1977: 295), emphasized the substantial equality of political resources.*

III. The New Deal and the Cold War as Backdrops: Liberal Pluralism's Focus on the Status Quo

According to Harry Elmer Barnes, writing in the 1921 *American Political Science Review*, both Cole and Laski – besides searching "for some method of social improvement" – could be given credit for having played a part in that "cardinal contribution of sociology to politics": the interpretation of government as the "agency" through which interest groups either "realize their objects, or effect ... (an) adjustment of their aims with the opposing aspirations of other groups". However, Barnes also contended that the "most thorough and comprehensive exposition" of that view could be found not in the works of English pluralists or guild socialists, but in Arthur F. Bentley's *The Process of Government* (Barnes 1921: 495, 512).

Rejecting both individualism and institutionalism, Bentley in his 1908 treatise aimed at introducing the group as the central analytical category. Describing his effort as "strictly empirical ... 'positively' grasp(ing) social facts just for what they are", he went on to argue that every activity could be stated "either on the one side as individual, or on the other side as social group activity". In interpreting social processes, however, the former was "in the main of trifling importance", whereas the latter "is essential, first, last, and all the time" (Bentley 1908: 56, 176, 210, 214/215).

In the United States, Harold Laski's normative considerations were echoed, to a certain extent, by progressive thinkers such as Mary Follett – who argued that the economic philosophy of individualism had resulted in the "crushing of individuals", of "all – but a few" (Follett 1918: 170) – and John Dewey who, like Follett, called for the "positive state", contending that "a measure of the goodness of the state is the degree to which it relieves individuals from the waste of negative struggle" (Dewey 1927: 72; Follett 1918: 182, 184). For a "brief moment", it seemed as if American progressives and British socialist pluralists might join in "accept(ing) the pluralist agenda", and that there might be a realistic chance, after World War I, to construct "a new political and social order" (Stears 2002: 2/3, 261). However, concepts for industrial citizenship did not catch on. In the United States, corporations, "with the full support of Democratic and Republican administrations in Washington", pushed back industrial relations to the practices "of the late nineteenth century". In England, the guild socialist tendency all but disappeared after the trade unions' defeat in the General Strike of 1925. The British Labour Party, subsequently, subscribed to the nationalization, rather than to democratic control, of key industries (Stears 2002: 263, 268).

Still, the behavioral group approach propounded by Bentley, which Barnes judged "the most notable American contribution to political theory", was likewise "neglected" after Bentley's book had first come out (Barnes 1924: 493, 494 n. 18). Eight decades later, informed opinion continued to agree: Bentley's "immediate impact on the discourse of political science" was "minimal" (Gunnell 2004: 105). That situation would change, after a considerable number of pressure group studies had been published in the United States between World Wars I and II, and after the New Deal had finally established organized labor and organized agriculture as industry's "junior partners" in bargaining for political benefits. As more and more social interests organized and 'log-rolling' became the established legislative procedure, the "acceptance of groups as lying at the heart of the process of government" was judged conceptually "unavoidable" (Truman 1951: 46).

For David Truman who, echoing Bentley, would state that "we do not, in fact, find individuals otherwise than in groups", Bentley's analysis had served as "the principal bench mark" (Truman 1951: IX, 48). However, the political system, according to Truman, was not merely accounted for "by the 'sum' of organized interest groups". He included constitutionalism, civil liberties, and representative techniques such as the "rules of the game" among the norms according to which organized groups had to operate. Otherwise, they risked bringing large, still *un*organized "potential" groups into action, whose widely held attitudes and values Bentley had termed the system's "habit background" (Truman 1951: 51, 159, 524; Bentley 1908: 218).

In its entirety, the group concept resembled a modified marketplace model ('interest-group liberalism', in Theodore Lowi's term): "The notion of individual competition is replaced by a network of organizational competition ... This makes for a system of countervailing powers" (Apter 1977: 312, 314/315). That "central ingredient of a stable pluralist democratic system" (ibid.: 355/356), countervailing power, was supposedly guaranteed by a "natural self-balancing factor ... almost amount(ing) to a law" – in other words, Adam Smith's 'invisible hand' in new clothes: "Nearly every vigorous push in one direction stimulates an opponent or a coalition of opponents to push in the opposite direction" (Milbrath 1955: 365; see also Kornhauser 1961: 130). Resulting from ever-present counterbalancing tendencies, "tam(ing), civiliz(ing), ... and limit(ing) power to decent human purposes", competing "multiple centers of power" were supposed to resolve conflicts "to the mutual benefit of all parties" (Dahl 1967: 24).

The group theorists' 'analytical' (Latham 1952: 9) or 'sociological' (Lijphart 1968: 2n.) pluralism, while claiming to disregard considerations of a normative kind, was admittedly biased toward group leadership. It was, in fact, an elite model, according to which leaders of associations conducted the process of organized pressure and bargaining, thereby "control(ling) each other" (Dahl/Lindblom 1953: 23, 325/326). Control *among* leaders, however, provided but one significant attribute of the political process. A second was control *of* leaders by means of periodic elections, holding them accountable to party or interest group members, and to the electorate at large. "Civic trust in leaders, and leaders' responsiveness to potential interest group claims might be expected to do the rest" (McLennan 1995: 35/36).

The Cold War confrontation encouraged the introduction of a more or less explicitly normative element into the concept. The rise of fascism and, more importantly after 1945, of communism were interpreted to demonstrate the dangers of mass movements. Because in Western political systems leaders were assumed to have been "socialized into the dominant values ... of industrial society", politics of group leadership were supposed to ensure moderate, rational conflict, serving as a demarcation line domestically against radicalism and the "irrationality and chaos" of mass politics, internationally against totalitarianism (Rogin 1967: 10, 15; see also Nicholls 1974: 25).

Liberal pluralism "portrayed capitalist democracy in a favorable light and gave it a little theoretical apparatus which discriminated nicely between this system and other systems with which we as a nation were in rivalrous relations" (Douglas Rae, quoted by Merelman 2003: 50/51). Put otherwise, the static descriptive (see Rothman 1960: 31/32) and the anti-totalitarian normative dimension blended in a manner to ensure the "astonishing career" (Steffani 1980: 9) of pluralism as a "public philosophy" which "public men" grew accustomed to use rather instinctively both as guideline and justification for their policies (see Lowi 1967: passim, and id. 1979: 51 ss.). Substantiation of the argument is provided by two not untypical examples, both a decade and a continent apart: When the Portuguese "revolution of carnations" seemed to veer to the left during 1974/75, the European Community's Council of Heads of State and Government declared "that the EC, because of its political and historical tradition, can grant support only to a pluralist democracy" (Commission 1976: 8). And in the United States, the National Endowment for Democracy (NED) was set up by the early 1980s with a view to promoting "American-style pluralist societies" (*New York Times* 1984: B 10).

In politics as in political science, "pluralism's flexibility, adaptability, terminological simplicity" (Merelman 2003: 117; also ibid.: 123) helped to spread the discourse. The quote by Winfried Steffani referred to West Germany, where every major political party, as Steffani showed, professed to back "free and pluralist democracy". In post-World War II Germany, the experience by many of intellectual exile in the United States during the Nazi regime had favored the emergence of a 'neo'-pluralist concept largely analogous to the American model (and indeed influenced by David Truman's argument; cf. Eisfeld 1998: 394/395). The approach was judged in retrospect "probably the most important product of the early stage of (West-German) political science" (Blanke et al. 1975: 76):

Not only could 'neo'-pluralism lay claim to putting the theory of parliamentary democracy on a new footing; it also won wide acceptance beyond the discipline of political science. Explicitly substituting totalitarianism – "the construct beyond the 'Iron Curtain' and the Wall" (Fraenkel 1968: 165) – for monism as the principal counterpart to pluralism, it also served as a perfect Cold War term. Ernst Fraenkel who had initially embraced the notion with some hesitation (cf. id. 1957: 236), only to push it the more vigorously later, bluntly professed that neo-pluralism was "fighting – to say nothing of Hitler's shadow – the much less faded shadow of Stalin" (Fraenkel 1968: 187). The simplified 'neo'-pluralism/totalitarianism dichotomy would soon prove a major reason for questioning the model (Eisfeld 1972: 86; Kremendahl 1977: 209/210).

Liberal pluralists usually conceded that income, education and status were apt to determine, to a considerable extent, political activity, including control of leaders and access to government (Truman 1951: 265; Dahl/ Lindblom 1953: 315). They also noted that these resources were not merely unequally distributed between business and labor (Truman 1951: ibid.), but that the system offered "unusual" opportunities for "pyramiding" such resources into structures of social power (Dahl 1963: 227). However, the prospects for "citizens weak in resources" to influence government – principally by associating with others – were not seriously questioned, because "probably no resource is uniformly most effective in American politics" (Dahl 1967: 378; see also id. 1963: 228). *Generally, it was formal equality of opportunity which liberal pluralism emphasized.*

IV. Democratizing Economy and Society: Dahl's and Lindblom's Transformation of Liberal Pluralism

During the late 1960s, when the Cold War had thawed, when radical dissent over ever more massive American bombing in Vietnam brought the "armies of the night" converging on Washington and Lyndon Johnson's vision of a Great Society succumbed to the exigencies of the same Vietnam War, the then president of the American Political Association felt bound to note that political scientists, "in some considerable measure, (had) worn collective blinkers". Their restricted vision had prevented them from recognizing major flaws in current interpretations of democracy, making them susceptible to "governmental interpretations of American interests ... both at home and abroad" (Easton 1969: 1057). David Easton therefore supported a rearrangement of research priorities "in the light of a better understanding of own value assumptions", including the construction of political alternatives, rather than "uncritically acquiesc(ing) in prevailing politics" (id.: 1058/1059, 1061).

Robert Dahl and Charles Lindblom, having turned more skeptical and radical in their assessments, later explained their earlier commitment to the ongoing political system in sentences that read like a comment on Easton's statement: "The New Deal was not a remote historical episode. It provided grounds for thinking that reform periods would again occur with some frequency" (Dahl/Lindblom 1976: XXX; see also David Mayhew in a 1997 interview, quoted by Merelman 2003: 85: "Pluralism [was] a New Dealish philosophy"). In looking back on his career a few years earlier, German political scientist and sometime emigré Ernst Fraenkel likewise attributed his "development of a pluralist model of democracy" to "the experience of the 'Roosevelt

Revolution'" when labor and agriculture had been recognized as political players alongside business (Fraenkel 1973: 26).

Looking for ways to remedy what Dahl eventually would identify as the "dilemmas of pluralist democracy", Dahl and Lindblom singled out the large business corporation – the "corporate leviathan" (Dahl 1970: 117) – as the major target for structural, participatory reforms. To a remarkable extent, liberal pluralist thinking (unlike Laski's radical pluralism) had previously failed to diagnose and analyze economic constraints. No systematic consequences had been drawn from the acknowledgment that oligopoly, "the most frequent market form of modern (capitalist) economies", and the resulting monopolistic competition are "group phenomena" (Latham 1952: 5). Instead, as shown by the quotes included above, it had been maintained as a general supposition that "organization begets counter-organization" (Latham 1952: 31).

In a manner reminiscent of Harold Laski's earlier argument, but more systematically, Dahl and Lindblom now focused their analysis on the transformation of the privately owned and managed firm into the joint-stock company, the ensuing divorce between property and control, and the exercise, by the large corporation, of power comparable to that of states: "The small family enterprise run by its owner became the large enterprise in which operation was separated from ownership. The ideology of the private enterprise of farmer and small merchant was transferred (, however,) more or less intact to the big corporation ... (even if) nothing could be less appropriate than to consider the giant firm a *private* enterprise" (Dahl 1970: 119/120; also Dahl/ Lindblom 1976: XXVIII).

Nothing could be less appropriate, because business corporations – with regard to sales, assets, numbers of employees, the impact of their pricing, investment, and financing policies – had developed into *social and public* institutions, "political bodies" with an "internal government". As Dahl and Lindblom went on to emphasize, because of the persisting application of the ideology of private ownership to the large corporation "excessive weight (is given) to the particularistic interests of managers and investors" (Dahl/ Lindblom 1976: XXIX). The ensuing "privileged position of business" – and of "corporate executives in particular" – involves the capacity to distort public policies, or – should undesirable measures nevertheless be legislated – to contract out from under the effects of such legislation (Dahl 1982: 40 ss.). Thus, it "restrict(s) polyarchical rules and procedures (i.e. those approximating democracy) to no more than a part of government and politics, and ... challenge(s) them even there" (Lindblom 1977: 172, 190).

Suggesting that corporate "rulers" were subject neither to effective internal control by stockholders, nor to adequate external control by governments and markets, Dahl went on to propose a determined effort at further democratization – the "enfranchisement" of blue- and white-collar employees, realizing industrial self-government in the sense originally propounded by Harold Laski (Dahl 1982: 199, 204; Dahl 1989: 327 ss., 331/332). Dahl's position may not have been one "with any clear sense of its connections to the past" (Gunnell 2004: 235), even if in one instance he did acknowledge that, by the late 1930s, he had "read Laski", and that he and Lindblom "were familiar with the British ... ideas about pluralism" (Dahl 1986: 234, 282 n. 11). At any rate, the following quote might have come straight from Laski's *Grammar of Politics*:

- "To say that people are entitled to the fruits of their labor is not to say that investors are entitled to govern the firms in which they invest" (Dahl 1989: 330).

In Germany, a distinct "Laski School" (Detjen 1988: 63) had emerged by this time whose exponents, not unlike Dahl and Lindblom, argued in favor of "democratizing" the economy and, by fusing everyday "social" with "political" activity, developing perceptions and qualifications conducive to a more participatory political process (Eisfeld 1972: 21, 103; Bermbach/Nuscheler 1973: 11; Nuscheler 1980: 158/159). Pointing to the legitimating functions of the established pluralist discourse (Eisfeld 1972: 85/86; Bermbach/Nuscheler 1973: 10; Nuscheler 1980: 157), these writers also took pains to emphasize the inequality of political resources and, consequently, the limited representativeness of interest groups – pluralism "as a smokescreen for the realpolitik of elite accommodation" (Garson 1978: 157).

In the United States, the indictment of pluralism's egalitarian shortcomings by Dahl and Lindblom amounted to an "internal transformation" of the concept by two of its leading exponents (McLennan 1995: 4). Earlier critiques of the model's shortcomings had served as forerunners. Liberal pluralists had argued that cross-cutting pressures from overlapping group memberships affecting an individual were apt to promote "compromise through bargaining" (Truman 1951: 162/163, 166; Dahl/Lindblom 1953: 329). In the last instance, conflicting group loyalties supposedly served to advance "a high degree of liberty *and* consent" (Kornhauser 1961: 80). Allusions to political apathy had at least surfaced as a quite different possible outcome in the texts of both Truman and Dahl/Lindblom, even if neither had pursued the implications for democratic politics. A more detailed examination based on the same empirical findings would conclude that apathy, in practice, may either mean frustration, the "compartmentalization of simultaneously maintained loyalties", or "non-rational adaptation" – in other words, inertia and docility (Mitchell 1963, as quoted by Lijphart 1968: 11; Eckstein 1966: 72 ss.).

Severe doubt was thus cast on the supposedly democratic effects of liberal pluralism's central provisions. In addition, it was demonstrated that the entire model of group interaction "breaks down" (Rothman 1960: 23) if the concept's reasoning is reversed, as Truman had done in his book's concluding chapter. Defining, as will be recalled, *potential* groups in terms of "widely held", but "unorganized" interests (i. e. attitudes), Truman had singled out "multiple memberships" in these *potential* groups as the political system's "balance wheel" – in other words, the polity's decisive factor (Truman 1951: 512, 514). He had thereby resorted to a "deus ex machina" which could be brought in "for any purpose" (Rothman 1960: 23; see also Lowi 1979: 37).

Closer examination of the countervailing-power hypothesis shattered a final corner-stone of liberal pluralism. Even if this particular debate largely focused on the specific economic form given to the argument by John Kenneth Galbraith – according to whom "in the typical American market", private economic power was supposed to generate "the countervailing power of those who are subject to it" (Galbraith 1956: 125, 151, 182) –, still it had something generally applicable to say about the "romantic" attribution of "proxy-mindedness" to organizational oligopolies (Stigler 1954: 9/10). The concept, as was shown, basically amounted to a philosophy of "perpetual stalemate" which made it conservative in impact and undemocratic in action (McCord Wright 1954: 14; see also Lowi 1967: 20). In addition, the critique of the countervailing-power scenario suggested other analyses that depicted today's large-scale organizations as "unwieldy", "unresponsive" – to changes in their environments – and "insensitive" – to the need for flexibility. Cumbersome and immune to internal or external control, they were charged with generating alienated, angry and/or apathetic individuals who "feed streams of hostility and aggressiveness into both domestic and international affairs" (McClelland 1965: 268).

If the liberal variety of pluralism emerged distinctly frayed from the melee, the debate had also emphasized the normative challenge posed by pluralism's inherent anti-monist, anti-hierarchical, participatory implications. Radical pluralist propositions, such as those put forward by Robert Dahl from the mid-1970s, have consequently merged into the larger, more comprehensive debate on democratization, a "spill-over" of democratic norms onto economy and society. The attribute "political" has thus been reconceptualized, now relating to any form of group decision-making. Pluralist democratization would be intended to make "all societal sectors more responsive to their members" and thereby society as a whole "more receptive" to its own pivotal value – the norm of political equality (Etzioni 1968: 6).

Actual evidence is ambiguous as to what extent such visions of increased citizen competence and control might be accepted, internalized, or practiced by increasing segments of "consumption-oriented, acquisitive (and) privatistic" societies (Dahl 1970: 135). Experiences with isolated "participatory environments" do not automatically promote general orientations furthering broad social change in a more egalitarian direction (see Greenberg 1981). The present situation not only warrants further research, but more participatory experimentation. This seems unlikely, however, as democratic governance is being delegitimized under the impact of the increasingly "hegemonic" neo-liberal discourse accepted by governmental and market players alike who rival each other in "reinvent(ing)" and reorganizing the state "along the lines of private industry" as a "quasi-'enterprise association'" bent on cutting out-lays and proving competitiveness (Cerny 1997: 251, 256, 269; id. 1999: 2).

V. The Rise and Demise of the Neo-Corporatist Alternative

On top of the reemergence of radical pluralism, likewise taking "a less benign view of the democratic credentials of group politics" in comparison to liberal pluralists (Williamson 1989: 3), neo- or liberal corporatism was the second conceptual challenge to confront liberal pluralism during the early 1970s. By the mid-sixties, Stein Rokkan had already characterized "established" triangu-lar interest representation in Norway as "corporate pluralist" – labor, farming and business interests maintaining existing inequalities by conspicuously ex-cluding the unorganized from bargaining processes at the top, as "corporate pluralist" (Rokkan 1966: 105). Referring to the post-World War I involve-ment of organized business interests with public administrations in formulat-ing economic policies to "recast bourgeois Europe", Charles Maier had also used the term "corporate pluralism" to label such interplay (Maier 1974: 202 ss.; and id. 1975: 353/354, 543).

Neo-corporatists, with Philippe Schmitter and Gerhard Lehmbruch in the forefront, now focused more systematically on "institutionalized patterns" of policy formulation and implementation, in which organized business and or-ganized labor "cooperate(d) with each other and with public authorities" at the leadership level, controlling and mobilizing group members in a top-down process (Lehmbruch 1979: 150, 152; Panitch 1979: 123; Jessop 1979: 200). Such patterns required the involved leaders' commitment "to the overall le-gitimacy of the existing economic system", expressed in their willingness to "confin(e) themselves to demands", or to push for compromises, compatible with steady economic growth (Jessop 1979: ibid.).

Consequently, the neo-corporatist school of thought has insisted that (1) the "social and economic attributes around which interests organize" are "unequally distributed", (2) that such "socio-economic inequalities are re-flected in, and indeed reinforced by, the politics of organized interests", not least because (3) certain associations, particularly organized business and organized labor, are "granted privileged access" to governmental decision-making processes, (4) that political processes typically take the form of oli-garchically structured "interest intermediation" through a "closed process of bargaining" among leaders, "consciously or not" guided by efforts at promot-ing system stabilization, rather than interest maximization, and implying

(5) that involved associations, far from providing "valuable route(s) to participation", allow leaders "a regulatory role over their members" (Williamson 1989: 2/3, 68/69).

Proponents of corporatism and liberal pluralism alike have usually conceded that pluralist and corporatist arrangements more often than not may occur in mixed combinations, with (West) Germany providing a typical example (see, e.g., Beyme 1979: 238, 241; Streeck 1983: 279). Both varieties may, in fact, not perform too differently, considering what liberal pluralism had to say about bargaining among leaders and about the possible "pyramiding" of unequally distributed political resources.

Because trade union leaders may be expected to face particularly difficult tasks in "delivering their members" on agreements reached, the involvement of social democratic parties as predominant players *able to secure trade union support* has been considered a salient requirement of corporatist structures (Panitch 1979: 129/130; Jessop 1979: 207/208). As conclusively demonstrated by recent French and German experience, that condition was linked, in its turn, to a "fair-weather" situation of high economic growth, allowing for high real wages and high welfare benefits. The social democratic/trade union alliance was eroded when governments led by social democratic parties, accepting the notion of international "competitiveness" as the new social and economic orthodoxy, joined conservative administrations in attempts at mediating the consequences of globalization by the pursuit of deregulatory and privatization policies (Cerny 1997: 258 ss.). Recent developments have not borne out optimistic contentions that social democratic corporatism could be expected to remain politically and economically viable, because it provided not just a profitable, but also a stable "home for business" (Garrett 1998: 155, 157).

Corporatism, moreover, had always remained very much a "Europeanist" concept. With regard to the United States, observers continued to note "the strength of corporate business in the circles of decision" (Salisbury 1979: 213) even in the brief historical moment when the Nixon administration, during the early 1970s, seemed to be endorsing a corporatist solution. After that attempt had been abandoned, it was diagnosed that precisely because of that political strength, "and the concomitant weakness of labor", no genuine interest in such an arrangement existed on the part of the American business elite (Salisbury 1979: 228).

In present-day European polities, too, with "pro-market state intervention on the increase", and governments ever more determinedly "underperforming" with regard to regulation and public services, tripartite neo-corporatist arrangements including trade unions are replaced by a more assertive reemergence of "overarching" corporate hegemony (Cerny 1999a: 19/20). Or one could use the term 'corporate pluralism', preferred by Theodore J. Lowi in his preceding chapter, for a constellation which radical pluralists had diagnosed much earlier. By transferring production facilities and investment outlays between countries, shifting profits via transfer-pricing, and moving large amounts of liquid assets, multinational companies had long been able to opt out of the effects of national economic policies. The monetary and fiscal tools of legislative and governmental interventionism were already proving inadequate. With the progress of globalization, the mere threat by large transnational corporations of moving capital or economic enterprise out of the country has now gained so much in credibility that it "radically eats into the capacity" of legislatures. To comply with the demands of international investors and foreign competitive pressures, welfare states "must be traded down to minimal safety nets". Corporate hegemony means that "business has acquired veto power in economic policy" (Hirst 2004: 155; Ringen 2004: 4).

VI. The Ethnocultural Issue: Toward a Politics of Pluralist Inclusion?

In the increasingly multicultural Western-type societies which the migration component of globalization has entailed, mounting social inequalities and economic insecurities rank high among the factors which have been fueling the rediscovery of ethnicity as a source of belonging, of ostensible "certainty in an uncertain world" (Durando 1993: 26). As far back as three decades ago, analysts recorded a pronounced growth in tendencies by persons in many countries to insist on the significance of their groups' distinctiveness and, consequently, in the "salience of ethnic-based" (as against class-based, "which of course continue to exist") "forms of social identification and conflict" (Glazer/Moynihan 1975: 3, 7).

With these developments in mind, two arguments were advanced in favor of applying the norms of political pluralism to the problems posed by accepting ("recognizing") the cultural, religious, and linguistic heterogeneity of different ethnic groups, without inviting further societal segmentalization:

(1) Because pre-World War II strands of pluralist theory included the roles that associations play in individual self-development as a central theme, "striking similarities" were suggested to exist between these approaches and "the new theories of difference and identity" in a multicultural context. A 'reconstructed' normative theory of pluralism, it was argued, ought to provide for every individual's chance of both "engagement and disengagement with groups" to develop a "critical perspective" (Eisenberg 1995: 1, 3, 188, 190). Pluralism therefore should assess political systems not least "in terms of whether they contribute to the well-being of societal (i.e. ethno-cultural) groups".

(2) Because pluralism affirmed the belief "in the worth of diversity", the notion was held to "endorse", first and foremost, "*cultural* multiplicity" in the sense of a "cross-fertilized" rather than a "tribalized" culture (Sartori 1997: 60/61, 62).

Like political pluralism, the idea of cultural pluralism had also been inspired by William James' philosophy (see Menand 2001: 379, 388). When the term "cultural pluralism" was first introduced by Horace M. Kallen in 1924, immigrant subcultures were flourishing in the eastern United States, after nearly 15 million immigrants – mostly from southern and eastern Europe – had been admitted to the country between 1901 and 1920 (id. 2001: 381). Writing between 1915 and 1924, arguing against assimilationist pressures and "melting pot" conformity, Kallen offered his vision of a "commonwealth of cultures", a "federated republic" of different nationalities (Kallen 1924: 11, 116). Convinced that self-government was impossible without "self-realization", that the latter – in the sense of personal identity – hinged upon the assertion of ethnic differences, and that society's creativity would benefit from such heterogeneous strains, he proposed granting equal treatment to each ethnocultural tradition.

Cultural pluralism, as advocated by Kallen, evidently requires a measure of "structural" pluralism (Gordon 1975: 85, 88): To persist, ethnic groups, co-existing within the same society, must maintain some separation from each other. Policies of differentiated group treatment – e.g., affirmative action; official multilingualism; a composition of political agencies reflecting the existence of various ethnic groups – may work to reinforce both cultural and structural pluralism. To be effective, such policies need to show an awareness of the connection between cultural and economic power or, in other terms, between "workable" recognition and concomitant re-distributive measures (Phillips 2004: 71, 75). *Radical ethnocultural pluralism* – to avoid Milton Gordon's rather confusing term "corporate pluralism", meant to denote that the approach focuses on group rights (see Gordon 1975: 106; id. 1981: 182 ss.) –, *in analogy to radical political pluralism, emphasizes equality of condition.*

Such pluralism is in opposition to public policies that remain neutral toward ethnocultural differences: Neutrality implies that discrimination on ethnic grounds is legally prohibited, while benefits are provided according to individual eligibility. "The unit of attribution for equity considerations is always and irrevocably the individual" (Gordon 1981: 184). For that model, Gordon has retained the term liberal pluralism (see id. 1975: 105/106; id. 1981: 184). *Again, it is equality of opportunity which the liberal-pluralist approach emphasizes.*

Most of the relevant debate has been centering on the controversial relation existing between "pluralism and liberal neutrality", as one volume's title has summarized the central issue (see Bellamy/Hollis 1999). Should liberal principles and procedures be reinterpreted in scope and character, or – as maintained by, e.g., Chandran Kukathas – "is there insufficient reason to abandon, modify or reinterpret liberalism", for "its very emphasis on *individual* rights ... bespeaks ... wariness of the power of the majority over minorities" (Kukathas 1997: 230)? Would not any determined movement in the direction of group rights imply that "the individual's claim to be considered only as an individual, regardless of race, color, or national origin", will be irrevocably reduced (Glazer 1997: 137)? Might the acceptance of such rights, even inadvertently, work to endanger individual autonomy, to bar individuals from "opting out" of their group by adopting ideas and practices running counter to their ethnocultural heritage? Obviously, "groups as well as the state might violate ... individual rights" (Van Dyke 1976/77: 368).

More basically, where Bentley and Truman had favored the group as the primary unit, they were arguing in *analytical* terms. If the individual could always be found within groups, as both insisted, these were groups "of his *choice*" (Goulbourne 1991: 224). Conceptions of ethnocultural recognition and inclusion have, however, tended to assign a *normative* priority to their groups. The inadvertent result might consist in confining individuals to a premodern, neo-feudal "*ascribed* group definition and status" (Goulbourne 1991: ibid.).

Should not, consequently – and so as to avoid the promotion of "ethnic sectarianism" (Waldron 1997: 113) –, compromises rather than clear-cut solutions be sought? Bellamy, for one, has argued in favor of a politics of continuing "negotiated compromise" as a central feature of democratic processes guided by a vision of "non-domination, mutual acceptance and accommodation" (Bellamy 1999: 138). Such compromises might most likely be worked out in those cases where a "definite assessment of the oppression, discrimination and persistent exclusion of (a particular) group is possible" and the conflict with liberal principles thus "less sharp" (Galeotti 1999: 50). A pluralist politics informed by a spirit of both political participation and social justice clearly would concede such groups "some" political standing and "some" legal rights (Walzer 1997: 149). Clearly, then, elements of the corporate model should be introduced into liberal pluralism – but to what extent?

Available options (which, of course, may overlap) include legal protection and public funding for the expression of cultural pecularities; federalism as a form of self-government; finally group-based political representation, up to the complex arrangements of consociationalism, which have been attracting "increasing attention" as devices for "overcoming ethnic cleavages by political accommodation" (Stanovcic 1992: 368; see also Kymlicka 1995: chs. 2, 7). A general argument advanced in favor of such politics of recognition/inclusion has been that, while "the sense of being a distinct nation within a larger country" is indeed "potentially destabilizing", the "denial of self-government rights is also destabilizing, since it encourages resentment and even secession" (Kymlicka 1995: 192). Put in optimistic terms (and contrasting with Arthur Schlesinger's fears quoted at the outset), group-differentiated citizenship may result in the ability of "the plural state, unlike the liberal state, ... to offer an emotional identity with the whole to counterbalance the emotional loyalties to ethnic and religious communities, which should prevent the fragmentation of society into narrow, selfish communalism" (Modood 1999: 88).

Consociationalism, identical with a high degree of group-based political representation, includes the following basic elements (Lijphart 1977: 25): Considerable autonomy for each involved group in the management of its internal affairs; application of a proportional standard in political representation, civil service appointments, and allocation of financial resources; right of mutual veto in governmental decision-making; finally, joint government by an either official or unofficial grand coalition of group leaders.

In a case study of consociational democracy in the Netherlands during the 1950s and 1960s, a number of significant negative consequences had been spelled out – elite predominance, the arcane character of negotiations, a large measure of political immobilism (Lijphart 1968: 111, 129, 131). At an even more basic level, group autonomy (as already indicated above) may involve internal restrictions on the right of individual members "to question and dissent from traditional practices" (Kymlicka 1995: 154) – barriers which run counter to a liberal conception of minority rights: Groups "cannot act rightly in ways that disempower individuals ... from living successfully outside their bounds" (Galston 2002: 104).

In addition, immobilism – which Lijphart concedes to be "the gravest problem" (Liphart 1977: 51) – may lead to morally reprehensible deadlocks by "entrench(ing) an unjust status quo" (Bellamy/Hollis 1999: 75; see also Bellamy 1999: 127). The right of mutual veto in matters of public policy amounts to "concurrent", in John C. Calhoun's term, rather than numerical majority rule, and Calhoun's proposal for such a procedure was designed at the time to put America's pre-Civil War south in a position for "effectively block(ing) ... deliberation of the slavery question" (Bellamy/Hollis 1999: 74). Thus, expectations may not be met that a high degree of group-based political representation would contribute to a more vibrant democracy.

VII. The Challenge of Participatory Pluralism in a Globalizing World

The same issues have kept resurfacing during this overview of research on pluralism and democracy: A grossly unequal distribution of political resources; skewed power structures; a "centripetal politics" enacted – even before the advent of globalization – by a web of governmental-corporate centers proceeding in "partnership" (Ionescu 1975: 8/9). As a research framework for inquiring into these problems which will persist to haunt 21st century democracy, pluralism – it should be repeated – will be of continuing relevance if it reverts to the role of a "critical political theory" (Gettell 1924: 470). It must be critical, as it sporadically has been, about the status quo of concentrated economic and political power.

Such a radical pluralist approach may start from where early pluralists – Harold Laski and Mary Follett in particular – had left off in their attempt to define the social obligations of both business corporations and trade unions, and to surmount the unequal distribution of power between capital and labor (see Laski 1921: 97/98. 272 ss., 289 ss.; Follett 1918: 170). It may build on Robert Dahl's and Charles Lindblom's analyses and on Dahl's ensuing proposal to "achieve the best potentialities of pluralist democracy" by realizing what Dahl termed "a third democratic transformation": democratic internal government of economic enterprises (Dahl 1982: 47, 110, 170; id. 1989: 312, 327/328, 331/332).

Resorting to an analysis guided by a set of group-centered propositions, a radical pluralist approach is able to explain the segmentation of class structures into blue and white collar strata differentiated by vocation and attitude; the emergence of additional patterns of ethnocultural cleavages exacerbated by economic injustices; the continuing inequalities of economic influence and control, equivalent to so many structurally embedded participatory barriers; basic origins of social passivity and depoliticization; resulting unequal chances for the organized representation of interests; limits of redistributive and regulatory public policies before and since the onset of globalization; the weakening of state legitimacy due to the downsizing of public budgets and the reduction of resources available for allocation by representatives to constituents (e.g., Eisfeld 1986: 281/282; Putzel 2005: 12).

The normative challenge posed by pluralist analysis thus becomes apparent: At the very moment in history when the power and the accountability of democratic governance are literally bleeding away, when – consequently – the reasons "for high levels of citizen loyalty to the state or active commitment to the democratic process" are disappearing fast (Hirst 2004: 155), a determined effort at democratization merits to be once again put high on the agenda of our thinking about democracy.

Avigail Eisenberg[*]

Pluralism and the Politics of Diversity

For a brief period of time, in the 1910s and 20s, pluralism dominated philosophical and political scholarship in the Anglo-American world. In 1919, the preeminent philosophical journal, *The Philosophical Review,* devoted an entire issue to pluralism and drew together articles on pluralist metaphysics, pluralist psychology and pluralist politics. In the 1920s, a similarly esteemed journal in political science, *The American Political Science Review*, published several articles on pluralism by thinkers like Francis Coker, E. D. Ellis, and W. Y. Elliott on topics like 'the pluralist state' and 'The pragmatic politics of Mr. H. J. Laski'. Pluralism's adherents of this time managed to turn the notion of a unitary and sovereign state on its head. They displaced the conventional preoccupations of liberal individualism by introducing groups as intermediaries between the state and the individual. And just as political science was getting off the ground as a separate discipline, the pluralists argued for an interdisciplinary approach whose virtues depended on incorporating wisdom from sociology, philosophy, psychology in political analysis (Gunnell 1993: 105).

This was not to be the only heyday of pluralism. Post-Second World War America also witnessed a resurgence of what came to be known as 'political pluralism' mainly through the scholarship of Robert Dahl. Like the early pluralists, Dahl's work focused on the themes of power-sharing and group life as central components of democracy, though this time couched in the methodological trend of behavioralism in political science.

Upon the foundations of pluralism, a rich and diverse set of theories and debates were built up during the first decades of the 20th century and then again in mid-century. Yet, they appear to have had little if any lasting impact on contemporary debates in political science and normative theory where one might expect to find them.

This is partly due to the methodological trends of American political science, where rational individual choice dominated analysis by the end of the century and displaced the more groupist notions central to some renditions of pluralism. But in normative political theory, the occlusion of pluralist theory

[*]   I am indebted to Charles Blattberg, Rainer Eisfeld and Jock Gunn for their comments and suggestions. I am also grateful to Victor Muniz-Fraticelli for his excellent comments and infectious enthusiasm for pluralist ideas. Some of the thought-provoking suggestions I received from these reviewers could not be incorporated into this chapter but will be pursued in the future.

is more puzzling. By and large since the 1970s, pluralism is only mentioned in normative contexts either as a simple synonym for diversity (e.g. a 'plurality' of cultures) or to invoke the value pluralism of Isaiah Berlin. Value pluralism 'depicts a world in which fundamental values are plural, conflicting, incommensurable in theory, and uncombinable in practice – a world in which there is no single, univocal *summum bonum* that can be defined philosophically ...' (Galston 1999: 878).[1] But the debates in which value pluralists engaged are importantly distinct and in some cases only distantly related to those of political pluralists like Harold Laski, J. N. Figgis, G. D. H. Cole, Mary Parker Follett and Robert Dahl. Value pluralism is a normative theory about the nature of values, whereas political pluralism is a 20th-century theory about associational life in democracy.

Political pluralism shares some preoccupations about political power, group life and individual freedom with contemporary normative theory, particularly theories of multiculturalism and identity politics. Advocates of multicultural approaches to democracy have raised profound and controversial questions about the role of groups in democratic life. For example, Will Kymlicka has argued that protecting groups, like cultural and linguistic minorities, is connected to protecting individual well-being and specifically to securing the conditions necessary for meaningful individual autonomy. Cultural or linguistic communities provide their members with a context of values and options (what Kymlicka calls 'a context of choice') in which individual choices come to have meaning and value for the individuals who make them.

But group contexts are made fragile by a variety of circumstances. Communities become unable to provide their members with a rich set of options when they are threatened by persecution or domination or are simply too small and weak to sustain a social culture that is alive enough to provide members with a full range of meaningful options (Kymlicka 1995: 75). In these situations, which are fairly common in most societies, individuals either need to find another cultural context (i.e. they need to switch cultures) or they need protection and additional resources for their group. Switching cultures is often difficult. In any case, it works only if there are no barriers (e.g. discrimination, language, educational, or cultural barriers) preventing people from integrating. Also, sometimes, the expectation that individuals should switch cultures is unfair, as with indigenous peoples, and other national minorities whose communities are unable to provide a rich enough context of choice because of a history of unjust policies for which the majority is mainly responsible.

The protection of a context of choice, though inspired by a concern for individual well-being, may well require measures that protect communities,

---

1   See Galston 2005 for an analysis of the political implications of value pluralism. Also see Isaiah Berlin 1990.

especially minorities. According to Kymlicka, some ethnic and linguistic groups require protection through collective rights and other group-based measures and some groups need limited autonomy, because making decisions for themselves is the best and fairest way for them to protect their societal culture. This raises some fairly difficult questions when one considers a political world that is inhabited by commitments to uphold both individual and collective rights. For example, given the importance of groups to individual well-being, how should a multicultural democratic polity sort out conflicts between groups and their dissenting members? How should individuals be protected from groups that oppress them? And how should conflicts between different groups be sorted out?

These questions are similar, in some respects, to ones that shaped political pluralism, especially British pluralism in the 1910s and 1920s, and postwar pluralism in the 1950s. In this chapter I argue that the earlier, pre-WWII pluralists provided a richer set of conceptual resources on which to draw in thinking about the place of groups in democracies than did the post-war pluralists. This is because post-war pluralists conceived of pluralism as a system of interest-group interaction. They advanced a view of the individual as voluntarily associated with groups and of groups as instrumental creations to advance aggregate individual interests in the public sphere. Based on these ideas, post-war pluralists conceived of democracy in a way that avoided many of the key questions that theorists of multiculturalism and group-differentiated citizenship grapple with today. Contemporary democracies, in the Americas, Europe, Asia and Africa, are increasingly looking for guidance about how to structure the public sphere in order to respond fairly to groups where groups are understood to constitute individual identities and therefore not as instrumental collective contexts merely meant to facilitate the relation between individuals and the state. The strengths of political pluralism, I argue, are found in the pluralist notion that group life constitutes individual identity and that group life in democracy involves the need to balance the interests of individuals, groups and the state. This strength was diluted in the post-war period when pluralists advanced a view of groups as instrumental creations.[2] Below, I canvass some key pluralist ideas in order to point to the ways in which political pluralism might be helpful to contemporary democratic theorists of group life.

---

2   Many scholars writing about cultural diversity might have used the term pluralism to describe their research but did not focus on this kind of balance. In particular see Furnivall 1948, Kallen 1956 and Kuper 1969.

I. Groups as Persons in British Pluralism

Rather than starting from liberal premises, the early pluralists were liberalism's critics and their starting point was instead to defend the importance of groups against naïve individualism and absolute state sovereignty both found within liberal theories of Thomas Hobbes and John Austin. One of the most interesting contributions of these early pluralists was to transform the theories of group personality, initially found in the work of Otto von Gierke (1977) and F. W. Maitland (1936), into a practical and powerful attack on state sovereignty. Gierke and Maitland argued that theories of state sovereignty rested on the misguided idea that groups existed only at the sufferance of the state (Heiman 1977: 19). According to Gierke, most theories of sovereignty recognized groups as mere legal fictions which are controlled by the state to the extent that their very existence was said to depend on the state's concession or recognition of them. According to concession theory, if a group aroused the state's displeasure, it could be divested of recognition and lose its legal status.

Gierke argued that these ideas, which were foundational to absolutist theories of sovereignty, violated the real and moral sense in which groups have 'personality'. Groups, he argued, were real persons which existed "over and above the multiple individual persons of which they were composed" (Barker 1950: xxix) and regardless of whether or not they received state recognition. According to how the idea was employed by the British pluralists, because groups possess real personality, they have the 'right' to their legal personality. In the same way that individuals are treated unjustly when they are denied juristic status, a group is treated unjustly when the 'real personality' it possesses is ignored.[3]

The British pluralists were on the whole not very interested in the methodological holism of this German idealism. They wanted to use the idea of moral and group personality to defeat what they viewed as an overzealous, power-hungry state. Cole and Laski found Gierke's theories useful to argue against attempts by the British state to undermine the status and power of a growing trade union movement. The personality argument entered public debate early in the century as the result of the *Taff Vale* case of 1901 which held that, even though the law denied unions the full legal status of corporations, and thereby denied them legal personality, they could be treated as though they possessed personality for the purposes of being sued or otherwise being held legally responsible for the acts of their members. The case, given the

---

3   There was scholarly disagreement about the extent to which Gierke was willing to take this metaphor. Ernest Barker (1950), for instance, argued against both the idea that groups possess 'real personalities' and the idea that Gierke thought they did in the same sense that individuals do.

disadvantages it posed for unions, came in for criticism from most social democrats except for those, like Laski, who took the doctrine of group personality somewhat seriously. Laski saw *Taff Vale* as ultimately leading to a more extensive set of group rights and duties for unions. And the fact that the personality of unions was recognized independently of explicit legislation affirmed what in his mind was a more socially grounded notion of sovereign power and how it is distributed. "As a matter of law", he argued, "government may possess unlimited power; in actual fact there will always be a system of conditions it dare not attempt to transgress" (Laski 1921: 22), such as, for instance, defiant trade unionists who pose challenges to state-imposed restrictions on picketing and strikes, or religious dissenters who historically played an important role in shaping the state's authority (Laski 1917: 136–137).

As with the communitarian notions which came to dominate liberal criticism in the 1980s, one challenge all of these pluralists encountered was in explaining how, on one hand, individual liberty was reconciled with these collective group-based rights (which, remember, had a legal and *moral* basis), and, on the other hand, how groups with their real personalities co-existed peacefully with each other.

In terms of sorting out the relation between groups and individuals, the pluralist position varied considerably, in fact to the point that it is difficult to say there was a position at all. Figgis barely mentions the individual in his major work on pluralism, *Churches and the Modern State*, except initially to justify his focus on groups. The individual "begins always as member of something ... his personality can develop only in society, ... I do not mean to deny the distinctness of individual life, but this distinction can function only inside a society" (Figgis 1913: 88–89). Pluralism was primarily a means by which community life was sustained, and Figgis was particularly interested in using the resources of pluralism to justify the legal protection and accommodation of the Catholic Church. To deny the Church recognition of its personality "is of the same nature as the denial of human personality which we call slavery and is always in its nature unjust and tyrannical" (Figgis 1913: 42).[4]

In contrast, Cole wanted none of these obscure German ideas about group personality that attracted his fellow pluralists. He upheld strictly individualist standards by insisting that associations act legitimately only when they adopt aims and goals "which affect all ... members more or less equally and in the same way" (Cole 1920: 96). At the same time though, and in response to the question of how groups peacefully coexist, Cole embraced a form of corporatism in which he believed the state to have a minor role. All the associations that Cole had in mind were limited to specific functions, including the state, whose function was limited to addressing matters on which the citizenry had 'an identity of interests'.

---

4   In other writings, Figgis displays a more liberal disposition towards groups. See Nicholls 1994.

He also believed that these functional associations would peacefully co-exist, each performing its function, and thereby fulfilling individual needs and interests. Associations that are disruptive of this social harmony posed a problem which Cole seemed aware of, though unable to resolve satisfactorily. He argued in favor of the disruptive influence that trade union activity was having on the British state, yet provided no assessment of when and how disruptions to social harmony were good and beneficial and when or how they should be resisted. As a result, his theory was short on useful normative guidance in relation to inclusivity and diversity.

Laski might have found a comfortable position in the context of these alternatives. But his theory never managed to bring together all of its promising elements. On one hand, he was a strong advocate for group personality and, from this starting point, developed a polyarchic approach to sovereignty and power. This is reflected not only in his theory about the nature of the state, in his belief that groups possess 'personality', and in his comments on *Taff-Vale*, but also in his discussion of individuals as 'bundles of hyphens' whose natures are largely determined by their associative ties (Laski 1921: 170).

On the other hand, Laski had no illusions or hopes, as did Cole, about the harmonious interactions of groups and, to the contrary, understood group competition to have important virtues. In this vein, he wrote about pluralism as a safeguard for individual liberty, and about federalism as a practical example of pluralism, in a manner that echoed the ideas of Lord Acton some years earlier and would be echoed in the ideas of Pierre Elliott Trudeau many decades later: "The secret of liberty", he argued, "is the division of power. But that political system in which a division of power is most securely maintained is a federal system; and, indeed, there is a close connection between the idea of federalism and the idea of liberty" (Laski 1921: 86–87).[5]

Moreover, a pluralistic state, where groups are free to pursue their own vision of the good life, is one where diversity itself will give full play to the 'creative impulses of men', and act as a constant reminder of the importance of freedom. But here, pluralism does not merely function as a source of information for the state. Rather, Laski seems to be arguing that when groups are free to pursue their own conception of the good life, they end up contributing different perspectives to the public sphere and these perspectives expose the biases within mainstream society.

A politics that recognizes group-based differences will emerge from the pluralistic state and this will cure citizens of 'undue localism' and expose publicly the ways in which different notions of freedom and rights are impor-

---

5   Like those of Acton and Trudeau, Laski's ideas on federalism were developed partly in thinking about Canadian federalism and corresponding with Lord Haldane, one the members on the Judicial Committee of the Privy Council (JCPC), which acted as Canada's 'supreme court' until 1949. The JCPC was responsible for writing many decisions crucial to shaping Canadian federalism. See Laski 1923. Also see Schneidermann 1998: 76.

tant for different kinds of groups. As Laski illustrates the point, "it is surely ... significant that the movement for the revival of what we broadly term natural law [and thereby the recognition of group personality] should derive its main strength from organized trade unionism" (Laski 1919a: 573). So a pluralist state provides the best guarantee for rights because only in such a state do people understand what it means to have their rights denied. They know this, not because some people are explicitly segregated by law (although there was that too), but because their differences expose the way in which mainstream guarantees suit the interests of some quite well and unfairly deny the interests of others.

The insight here is profound when considered in light of multicultural arguments which have triggered similar notions about how to reconcile the protection of individual rights with collective rights. Although collective rights are often treated as a departure from individual rights, the need for collective cultural rights rests on the understanding that basic individual rights and freedoms are sometimes best guaranteed by protecting groups. The idea is that individuals who are members of minority cultures will not enjoy equal opportunities compared to members of the majority as long as everyone's opportunities are structured in a manner biased in favor of supporting the values and lifestyles of the majority.

To take a simple example, members of a linguistic majority have easier access to jobs and educational programs within their society than do linguistic minorities just in virtue of the fact that they speak the language. Similarly, insofar as the majority's cultural, linguistic, or religious values have the effect of structuring opportunities (in implicit, if not explicit, and indirect ways, as in the case of language), minority groups are thereby disadvantaged.

In this light, to get beyond a highly abstract account of 'the right to equal opportunity', to 'freedom of association', to 'freedom of religion', etc. depends on understanding what impairs these freedoms for different groups. Just as the members of trade unions, in Laski's time, argued that freedom of assembly entails the 'right to strike', cultural and religious groups have argued that their basic rights to equal treatment is denied when they are social, economically or even legally penalized for wearing yarmulkes, turbans, or head scarves, enjoying a day of rest on their Sabbath, or otherwise following their religious and cultural customs.

While these arguments tend to raise the concern that, once recognized, cultural rights will have no limit, the basic point of these arguments is to show that the scope and limits of all rights and liberties is unknowable without understanding the nature of the groups themselves and specifically understanding what being deprived of or enjoying freedom means to those who are members of different kinds of groups. In this sense, some multicultural theorists today also argue that groups are conduits of freedom because they provide the substantive means to understand what abstract ideals, like individual liberty, amount to in practice.

The question that remains for Laski is how can individuals enjoy freedom apart from their associations and free of their community's constraints? Laski's work didn't resolve this problem (nor does the work of multicultural theorists). In fact, when pressed, he either stressed the importance of group personality (early in his career) or the need for individual freedom from the constraints of dominating associations (later on). By the 1930s, he represented rights as the ultimate refuge for the individual, "for in any system of rights, the ultimate uniqueness, and therefore isolation of the individual is the basic starting point" (Laski 1925: 95); and further, rights "safeguard our uniqueness in the vast pressure of social forces" (Laski 1925: 94). Nowhere in his work does he recognize the possibility that strong guarantees for individual rights might, in some circumstances, jeopardize groups (including trade unions).

Yet, at the same time, his argument points out interesting dimensions of the tension between groups and individuals. One dimension is that groups (especially progressive groups committed to social equality) are often the conduits of freedom because they contribute different perspectives to public debate about what freedom entails.[6] Moreover, their perspectives are derived from a group-based experience. They are not derived from the experiences of 'unhyphenated' and identical individuals, but rather arise from the experiences of individuals who are situated within group contexts. Groups create a perspective. Pluralist politics (or the recognition of group personality) places this perspective within a broader societal perspective and thereby cures individuals of undue localism.

Another interesting dimension is the creative tensions that group conflict and competition generate. Laski was clearly thinking about particular kinds of groups, especially provinces or states within federal arrangements like those in Canada and the United States, rather than the ethnic rivals of deeply divided societies. Dividing power and sovereignty was a means to healthy competition for the loyalties of citizens. He also realized that federalism, because it divided power, could erect obstacles to the development of large-scale cooperative projects, like social welfare programs (Laski 1923). Laski's response to this problem, at least with reference to the Canadian case, was to argue for more pluralism: that is, functional rather than merely territorial pluralism. In this respect, he argued against the general wisdom on the Left, that a division of powers threatened some kinds of cooperative projects and that a

---

6   Of course, this is not only Laski's insight. Trade unionism, socialist and communist political parties were strong advocates of individual rights in Canada, Britain and the United States in the 1910s and 1920s largely because they were so frequently denied these rights in their efforts to organize collectively and attract votes. For an excellent study on this era of political organizing in Canada, see James forthcoming, especially chps 2 and 3.

strong central state was, in particular, an asset to a strong social welfare system.

The ideas and theories of British pluralism were not intended to solve problems related to ethnic diversity. But at the same time, British pluralism contains some insights familiar to these later debates. One such insight is that individual well-being and liberty is protected by protecting group-based life. Group personality, in a legal and moral sense, was a distinctive idea within pre-Second World War pluralist theory. It amounted to something very much like collective rights to autonomy within particular areas of life. The pluralists argued that because individuals live their lives through groups and are loyal to groups, groups enjoy and ought to enjoy, for moral reasons, a form of sovereign power. The state is thereby obligated to recognize the 'personality' of groups.

From this starting point, pluralists attacked the notion of the absolutist state on the one hand, and the narrowly-conceived idea of individualism on the other hand. Groups were viewed as the means by which individual rights were best protected, and competition amongst groups, if structured properly, was seen as a means to ensure individual liberty. What was less clear is where the state derives its power from, especially power to ensure that rights are enforced consistently, to settle conflicts between groups and individuals, and to coordinate activities amongst groups. The pluralists did not agree about whether the state should be seen as an umpire or merely another association in competition with the rest. In any case, this aspect of their work was not to survive beyond the interwar years, until some parts of it were picked up by the American pluralists in the post-Second World War period.

II. Post-War Pluralism and the Renaissance of Individualism

Although little attention is devoted to the work of Figgis, Cole and Laski today, in the 1950s many American political scientists were well versed in their work. Robert Dahl, who was the leading proponent of post-war pluralism in the United States, acknowledged the influence that Laski had on his own thinking about pluralism (see Dahl 1986: 281–282 n. 11) and, while a student at Yale in 1936–7, studied under men like Francis Coker, who were greatly influenced by Laski's arguments (see Eisenberg 1995: 96). Like these earlier pluralists, Dahl's pluralism began with an attack on the going theories of the state – in Dahl's case, the theory that a corporate-industrial elite controlled the American state (Dahl 1958). Dahl married the notion that power was distributed pluralistically to the empirical agenda amongst political scientists of the time which required that politics be understood in terms of the actual activity or behavior of individuals and groups. The post-war variant of pluralism showed that, in terms of measurable behavior and activity, political power is distributed pluralistically (i.e. not concentrated in a ruling elite), and group interaction is the definitive feature of democratic politics. Yet, at the same time, post-war pluralists conceived of groups primarily as 'interest groups', that is, as voluntary associations, with, on some accounts, none of the 'personality' that British pluralists found nor, indeed, any purpose other than the advancement of individual interests. Groups were aggregates of interest-driven individuals which safeguard liberty because they compete for political resources with other groups.

Dahl described democratic governance as a process that is set in motion when individuals who are affected by a given issue come together to form groups in order to voice their interests in the political process (Dahl 1956, 1961, 1967). These groups compete, negotiate and compromise in the political process with other groups. They advance their agendas by building coalitions and aggregating their resources. No group can monopolize all the resources partly because no one kind of resource dominates all the others. Coalition-building is thereby crucial to democracy because no group can succeed at advancing its agenda unless it teams up with other groups to form coalitions (Dahl 1961: 223–228), and in forming these coalitions, groups must negotiate and compromise with each other.

Political power is distributed pluralistically in the democratic state partly as a consequence of how individuals team up to form interest groups and partly because institutions themselves compete for resources and influence. According to post-war pluralism, public institutions interact with each other much in the same way as interest groups interact, by competing for resources in order to advance their interests.

Pluralists were fully aware that the American constitution allocated special powers to the courts, Congress and the President's office to affect public policy. But they argued that constitutional rights were powerless and meaningless unless the institutions and groups that championed them engaged in the sort of competition and coalition-building characteristic of the rest of the political process. As Dahl put it, "[a]cting solely by itself with no support from the President and Congress, the Court is powerless to affect the course of national policy" (Dahl 1967: 167–168).

The push and pull of regular interest-group politics was part of the larger democratic idea of pluralism, which included the constitutional checks and balances of the American political system. Individuals interact with other individuals to join groups, groups interact with each other to form coalitions, and institutions like Congress, the Supreme Court and the Presidency rely on coalition building with other institutional actors in order to advance their agendas. The direction and development of American democracy, Dahl argued, is determined, not by a "logically conceived philosophical plan", such as that contained in the U.S. Constitution, but by the practical democratic politics of coalition-building within a particular historical context with particular actors (Dahl 1967: 22).

In the 1970s, numerous scholars were criticizing this pluralist idea of democracy by claiming that it ignores and even inverts the principles of constitutional democracy. It was accused of giving short shrift to discussions of the common good, considerations of justice and right, and the plight of groups that are marginalized in the 'rough and tumble' of political competition.[7] Pluralists were criticized for suggesting that democracy rests on the political ascendancy of the more *persuasive* claim or powerful interest, that is, the claim or interest that attracts the most support of groups teamed up in coalitions, rather than the one that is guaranteed by the constitution to be most fundamental. The critics contended, *pace* post-war pluralism, that democratic politics should not treat all claims – including basic rights – *as though* they are interests which are appropriately the subject of political competition. Democracy at least requires the *prima facie* protection of political equality.[8]

In the 1990s, and in much the same spirit as these critics, Iris Young described interest-group pluralism as a theory based on the self-interested pursuit of policy objectives which uses the client-consumer relation to replace the citizen-state relation. Because interest-group pluralism focuses on the role that groups, not citizens, play in democratic processes, it fragments the 'whole' citizen into various interests, each of which is represented by an interest group. Politics becomes nothing more than horse-trading amongst groups and, in particular, seems to have little to do with deliberating about or pursuing social justice (Young 1990: 190). Nor is the aim of interest-group pluralism to facilitate mutual understanding amongst groups. Under the guise of free interest-group interaction, democracy becomes a matter of aggregating resources as best one can for the pursuit of private self-interest.

In part, these criticisms capture one of the main innovations of the post-war variant of pluralism with respect to how individuals are related to groups. Post-war pluralism relied in part on a view that individuals were *contingently* and *instrumentally* related to groups in the sense that individuals were members of groups in order to advance their interests and they left groups (and coalitions dissolved) once their interests were served. Groups were thereby imagined to be fluid and ever-changing. And democratic politics based on the activities of these groups was also a shifting and flowing set of interactions amongst diverse groups and shifting coalitions. The kind of group that par-

---

7   Even Dahl recognized that the common good gets short shrift as groups vie for self-serving goals. See Dahl 1978: 199; also see McConnell 1966; and Lowi 1979.

8   On this point, the pluralists, or at least Dahl, conceded and suggested that a 'democratic creed', made up of tolerance and respect for political equality underlies the American system and sustains liberal and democratic values which guide pluralist politics.

ticipates in this vision of democratic pluralist politics, namely an 'interest group', is a particular kind of voluntary association whose purpose is largely instrumental and whose membership is in flux; self-interested individuals come and go from these groups depending on what suits their purposes.

But there is a tension here, which surely did not escape the pluralist's notice, between the idealized vision of group interaction and the political reality of group life in the United States at the time. While the voluntary interest group, which fits into the post-war democratic vision is certainly a player in democratic governance, it is not the only kind of group that participates in politics – not now and not in the 1950s.

For instance, the cultural, linguistic and religious communities that pre-occupy contemporary theories of multiculturalism are, importantly, unlike these voluntary, interest-driven associations. The membership of these more constitutive communities is not in such flux, their interests are not so contingently held, and their interest in group life exists, to a considerable degree, independently of the ability of their groups to influence state policy. Individuals usually 'join' their ethnic, religious, or linguistic communities by birth, they rarely leave, and if they do, they don't discard their membership lightly or completely.

In these senses, cultural groups are *constitutive* of an individual's sense of self and, though they give rise to interests, they are not 'interest groups' as understood using the post-war pluralist paradigm. Their interests are deeply held and difficult (although not impossible[9]) to compromise. As a result, the interests of these communities are not the sort of interests that can be fairly negotiated or compromised through a system of 'horse-trading' or without risking serious social conflict.

Nor, for that matter, does this post-war pluralist idea capture the sense in which individuals are 'members' of a class or a racial group both of which also have interests that compete for resources in democratic societies. Like ethnic and religious communities, the categories of race and class, which were central to political activity in the 1950s, are conspicuously left out of the post-war vision of group life in a democracy.

But perhaps 'left out' is not the best way to understand the post-war approach to these other groups and perhaps understanding the post-war lacuna in this way only serves to obscure what must surely be the most enduring ten-

---

9   There is a risk here of overdrawing the contrast between constitutive groups like ethnic or religious communities and contingent groups like voluntary associations and interest groups. Even in voluntary associations, individuals can be deeply committed to seemingly contingent interests such as saving an animal habitat or securing subsidies for the farm. And many constitutive interests, like adhering to controversial religious practices, are often amenable to compromise. The main point here though, is that post-war pluralists favored a particular conception of a group which is, in important respects, more like a group which is instrumental, voluntary and self-interested. The main point here is that this conception fails to capture the nature of most groups, whether voluntary associations or not.

sion within post-war democratic theory, namely the necessary illusion of the voluntary association.

One way of interpreting post-war pluralism, which is consistent with some of the criticism it received, is that it was not concerned with constitutive groups and interests. Rather, self-interested and voluntary groups were central and foundational to its conceptual approach to American democracy. The pluralists imagined democracy in terms of a fluid process of groups forming, coalescing, partially overlapping each other, and disbanding as they advance their interests through interacting, i.e. compromising and negotiating, with other groups. The *contingent* nature of the interests at play in this democratic process is a core feature of this vision and one upon which pluralist democracy strongly relied. In fact, within the pluralist rubric, the supposition was that the more passionately and rigidly interests are held (as one might suppose some religious or cultural interests) the less willing individuals (and the groups they formed) were to compromise or negotiate their interests. Interests that are held with passion are the basis of factionalism according to Dahl, following Madison (1787: ch. 1), and factionalism is, in many ways, the antithesis of pluralist democracy.

Yet (and here the tension emerges), pluralists were far from disinterested in these less voluntary and self-interested groups. Nor did they neglect the close ties individuals have to some group interests, including especially interests derived from religion, race and class. To the contrary, post-war pluralism derived a great deal of influence from studies which focused in part on groups that were not voluntary or self-interested. In these early studies, researchers would often take not of the voting behavior of individuals who were members of groups that were neither purely voluntary groups nor groups formed to advance the self-interests of their fleeting membership. Rather, the groups at the center of these studies were racial and religious minorities, including Catholics, Jews, Protestants, African Americans, and women.[10]

These cohorts are not the same as 'interest groups' *per se*. In fact, they were nothing like the ideal voluntary association. But this difference made little if any difference within the studies. The attitudes of individuals within unions and religious communities were analyzed side-by-side and compared. The attitudes of racial groups were assessed in the same way as the attitudes of party members. In fact, some studies addressed the obvious gap between these seemingly different kinds of groups by suggesting that, in some sense, all groups are voluntary.[11] For example, Campbell et al., in *The American*

---

10 For example, see Berelson, et al., 1954; Campbell, et al., 1964; Lazarsfeld et al., 1948.

11 Some voting studies were interested in the degree to which individuals identified with groups. The researchers surmised that the stronger the identification the more likely individuals would exhibit voting behavior typical of the group. In many of these groups, even membership in the most constitutive sort of group is portrayed as a kind of individual choice.

Voter asked respondents the following question: "Would you say that you feel pretty close to (e.g.) Negroes in general or that you don't feel much closer to them than you do to other kinds of people." (Campbell et al, 1964: 168). Union members, Catholics and Jews were asked the same question as a means to determine the degree to which they viewed themselves as embedded in their cohort. These questions showed that the role of these groups in the individual's life was much like the role of any other group – i.e. ultimately a matter of individual choice.

In a sense, the question of whether or not any particular group is thought of as more like a voluntary association, constitutive community, cohort, category or classification is a perennial problem for pluralism, if not for all political theory. But the point of this problem is not simply a matter of a particular theory advancing a correct or incorrect understanding of groups. The fact is that even the most constitutive communities have identities that are negotiable in some ways while, conversely, many voluntary and non-ascriptive associations are contexts where individuals develop some of their most profound and deeply-held attachments, values, and self-understandings. The question for any given pluralist approach is what does the approach require of groups in order for these groups to fit into the pluralist conception of democratic life.[12]

In the post-war pluralist account, if individuals could be represented as controlling their membership in their race, class, religion and culture, these groups could be represented as though they were voluntary. And if these groups were voluntary, then the interests they represented or advanced – i.e. whether these interests were constitutive of their self conception or contingent and a matter of self-interest – could all be treated as contingent. And if all interests were contingent, then none was exempt from the rough and tumble of interest group competition, negotiation and compromise characteristic of pluralist politics.

One way of thinking about this distinctive post-war conception of group life in democracy was that it left out all sorts of groups. A second way is that it misunderstood the different natures of groups. But a third, and far more likely understanding is that the post-war pluralists were fully aware of the diversity of groups interacting in American democracy and sought an approach that would enhances the benefits of group life to democracy while weakening its dangers. In other words, the post-war approach recognizes only some groups as likely participants in democratic life and recognizes groups as

---

12 As Victor Muniz-Fraticelli has suggested to me, early pluralists such as Maitland and Figgis, who recognized the deep and constitutive nature of group life, required that groups formally organize their affairs and incorporate themselves. The state is obligated to recognize group personality as legal personality. This way of thinking of about groups and of sustaining group life in democracy has some interesting parallels with work done on group life in religious associations and the common law. See, in particular, Réaume 1997.

primarily contributing to democracy of their rule in facilitating the relation between individuals and the state.

The view taken by the post-war pluralism, that religious, racial and class-based groups are like other interest groups, *is* a distinctive way of thinking about all groups in the context of democratic politics. Moreover, this conception of groups gives rise to guidelines for how all claims (including those crucial to sustaining group identities) ought to be treated in democratic processes, and how all groups (whether political parties, parent associations or cultural communities) ought to act if they wish to partake constructively in the democratic process. One such guideline, already mentioned above, is that groups which passionately hold on to their interests, in a manner that is (close to) uncompromising, are harmful to democratic politics. A second guideline is that because all groups are supposed to be (more or less) voluntary associations, groups themselves don't need protection. Voluntary associations are sufficiently protected through the individual rights of their members, particularly the rights of individuals to enter and exit associations. Individuals create groups (rather than, in some sense, being created by groups) to suit their purposes and, when they leave groups, groups disband.

In this sense, post-war pluralism ostensibly offers a conventional expression of liberal individualist values but with a group twist at least in terms of how political power is distributed in democratic society. Two broader features of this approach are especially worth noting.

First, the post-war pluralist approach stands in contrast to the ideas adopted in pre-WWII pluralist theories about the role that groups play in the individual's life. One way or another, most pluralists until the post-war period viewed groups as contexts for individual development whose importance existed independently of their role in influencing state policy as well as in relation to the state, i.e., in developing, expressing, and defending in the public arena values and attachments that were deeply held by individuals (see Eisfeld 1986). This is true not only of the British pluralists, but also of early American advocates of pluralism like John Dewey (1927) and Mary Parker Follett (1918). The crucial project for all of these early pluralists was to develop a democratic politics that would be conducive to group life so that individuals could enjoy full and deep attachments to their associations and communities. None of these early pluralists was naïve about the potential oppression that often accompanies such constitutive attachments. The purpose of pluralism in their minds was to address both the importance of groups for individual development and their potential to oppress individuals.

What happens then when these dimensions of group life are dropped from the pluralist equation?

The second feature of the post-war approach was that, in portraying all groups as though they were voluntary associations even when many groups were not, the project of pluralism no longer entailed ensuring that individuals, on the one hand, enjoy healthy community life, and, on the other hand, are protected from the potential oppression of their cultural or 'private' communities. Interest-group pluralism only makes sense as an approach to democracy if individuals are conceived to be voluntarily or contingently bound to the groups. If, to the contrary, groups are constitutive of an individual's sense of self, or for that matter, if they are viewed as possessors of separate 'personality', then a politics that pits groups against each other to compete for scarce resources in order to advance their interests risks being unstable, and, especially where minority groups are concerned, seems unfair. When group life is viewed as an important component of individual well-being independently of its role in influencing state policy, as it was in pre-war pluralism, then liberal-democratic politics has to involve finding a way to balance the interests and values of groups, and to work out a means by which individuals can enjoy a rich community life yet escape the oppression and restrictions that their communities might impose on them.

I am not suggesting here that the early pre-war pluralists solved these problems satisfactorily; but they recognized that these were the important problems that democratic governance in pluralistic societies faced. The post-war pluralists, in contrast, tried to undercut these problems by pretending that groups were voluntary associations, even though many were clearly not.

III. Pluralism and Identity Politics

The approach to group life in democracy which portrays all groups as voluntary associations even though most are not, and the guidelines for democratic governance that follow from this approach probably do not originate in post-war pluralism, or at least no evidence here suggests origins of this kind.

However, it is not difficult to find evidence that post-war pluralism strengthened this conception of groups possibly as a means to undercut the problems that racial and class-based groups posed for American democratic ideals at the time. In doing so, the post-war account also strengthened the commitment that only individuals, not groups, require state protection and recognition through rights, and that democracy involves a sort of compromise and negotiation for which some groups are poorly suited; that is, some groups make poor 'democratic citizens'.

It is interesting to think about the resonance of these kinds of commitments in democratic theory today. For instance, despite the fact that we live in an age of 'identity politics', cultural, linguistic and religious groups are often portrayed as unsuitable participants in democratic politics. Some critics of multiculturalism argue that when cultural or religious groups advance interests related to their deeply-held values in the public arena, democratic debate quickly disintegrates into social conflict. Some people argue that constitutive claims about 'identity' and other deeply-held values are too personal and too absolute to be amenable to the sort of compromise required of democratic politics (see e.g. Bader 2001 and 2004; Johnson 2000; Waldron 2000; Weinstock 2001).

The problem is not that the critics misunderstand or exaggerate the prospects for conflict amongst ethnic groups. Rather, the problem is that, like the post-war theories, many democratic theories today implicitly rely on an understanding of democracy which either excludes ethnic, religious, racial, and class-based groups or somehow converts these groups into voluntary associations, like other interest groups, by creating the illusion that they are voluntary even though they are not.

Some interesting examples that bear this out can be drawn from democratic theory, including the work of neo-pluralists who have self-consciously built on the resources of pluralist theories from the past. Consider two examples.

First, associational democracy is a theory that groups, including cultural, linguistic, and religious groups, ought to assume a large role in fulfilling social functions within a democracy. The ideas of associational democrats echo some of the thoughts developed by British pluralists, especially Laski's and Cole's social democratic visions of functional associations. But its advocates are decidedly on the side of post-war pluralism when it comes to the question of whether the groups that participate in democratic governance are voluntary. For instance, Paul Hirst described his approach to associational democracy as involving the central claim that "human welfare and liberty are both best served when as many of the affairs of society as possible are managed by *voluntary* and democratically self-governing associations (Hirst 1993: 112, emphasis added). Veit Bader similarly describes the 'core proposition' of associational democracy to be that "as many social activities as possible should be devolved to self-governing *voluntary* associations" (Bader 2005: 323, emphasis added). Associational democrats explicitly exclude non-voluntary associations from assuming a role in democratic governance.

Most theorists are unlikely to opt for such explicit exclusion given the widespread attention today to cultural and national minorities in democratic life. Yet, even where such diversity is the background against which democratic values are theorized, theorists are nonetheless drawn to relying on the illusion of the voluntary association.

Consider, in this respect, a second example of neo-pluralism developed in a recent study of American democracy by Amy Gutmann. Gutmann applies some of the resources of American post-war pluralism about the role of interest groups in democracy to her normative analysis of the role that identity groups, like religious and cultural groups, play in American democracy today.

On the one hand, Gutmann accurately comprehends the important differences between 'identity groups', which are central to multicultural theory, and 'interest groups' which are usually viewed as central to American democratic theory. People join identity groups because they identify with others and not primarily out of self interest, whereas they join interest groups because they share political interests which are instrumental and often based in individual self-interest (Gutmann 2003: 19).

Yet, despite having drawn this distinction, the examples Gutmann analyses of 'identity groups' introduce the same sort of ambiguity her definitions mean to address. Religious communities such as Sikhs and ultra-orthodox Jews are considered alongside groups such as the NAACP (National Association for the Advancement of Colored People), and an Israeli Jewish feminist association called Women of the Wall, both of which are groups that seek to advance instrumental goals (Gutmann 2003: 13 and 16). Moreover, Gutmann treats both types of groups as appropriately engaged in negotiating and compromising their 'interests' in the context of pluralistic and democratic politics.

One of the main arguments of the book, which is that identity groups play an important role in American democracy, is facilitated by this ambiguity where, in the end, there is little difference between so-called identity groups and more conventional interest groups. Why shouldn't they play an important role?

These examples, drawn from neo-pluralist approaches, are only a small part of a much broader tendency in democratic theory to eschew what has come to be known as identity politics by insisting that individuals are in control of their group life even though, in many cases, this is a completely unrealistic assumption. Gutmann's analysis shows an awareness that groups differ in terms of their instrumental and voluntary nature. But the democratic paradigm that she works with demands that this difference be ignored so that democratic interchange can work along the model that facilitates interest group interaction. This is a familiar pattern in democratic theory, including theories that focus on multiculturalism.

Consider a third example drawn from a broad range of multicultural approaches. In many analyses of multiculturalism, a favored method of addressing the potential for group oppression in the otherwise rich scholarly literature devoted to multiculturalism and minority rights is to insist that all individuals must have the 'right to exit' their identity-bearing groups. Exit rights are rights, such as freedom of association, that are meant to ensure individuals the freedom to exit oppressive associations. They act as a way of ensuring that tensions between individuals and groups are less likely to arise and that basic rights are guaranteed to all individuals regardless of their religion or culture (see Barry 2001: 146–149; Gutmann 2003; Kukathas 2003: ch 3; Spinner-Halev 2001 and 2005).

As with the post-war pluralist assumption that all associations are voluntary even though many are clearly not, the right to exit offers a convenient way of avoiding many of the most difficult issues about how to balance the role of groups with individual well-being in democratic societies.[13] These issues include, for instance, why some individuals have no desire to leave religiously insular, culturally segregated or indigenous communities and join the 'liberal mainstream', even when their communities seem confining.

Well hidden behind the right to exit are all the factors that impede individuals from leaving their communities when they want to. These factors have touched off debates which are especially controversial in the United States amongst western democracies. They involve questions about whether individuals who are members of minorities can 'exit' their communities in the absence of publicly-funded education, including linguistic training and acculturation, job training, integrative affirmative action programs, and strong guarantees against discriminatory treatment in the public and private spheres. They also involve questions about whether resources are equally accessible to women and to children who are often the most vulnerable minorities within minorities.

The right to exit is undoubtedly a way of gesturing towards these kinds of issues. But these are empty gestures unless the difficult issues are more directly confronted. The problem is that a reliance on the right to exit makes it easier not to confront these issues.

When exit rights are offered as a shortcut solution to resolving the tensions that arise between individuals and groups, they enhance the illusion that groups are voluntary associations. Groups that are voluntary associations are those from which individuals can exit; in other words the only reason why individuals stay in groups is because they don't want to exit.

But exit and this illusion of voluntariness often serve as a substitute for examining difficult questions about how to address the tensions that arise between individuals and groups and how to provide meaningful options for individuals whether they remain within their communities or not.

As in post-war pluralism, when democratic theorists today conceive of all groups as voluntary associations (or conceptually transform them into voluntary associations using the rights to exit), there is a sense in which they implicitly marginalize groups that cannot meet this standard. Liberal democracy becomes a system of governance best designed for groups that are voluntary associations and for individuals with the wherewithal, that is the language skills, education, the financial and social resources, to exit their communities. Groups which are not voluntary, and I have suggested that many groups included and accounted for in these studies are not, are democratic misfits and viewed as threats to democracy because they introduce group-based, identity-

---

13   The avoidance of these issues is especially well illustrated in Kukathas 2003.

bearing interests that are passionately and deeply held and that can lead to social conflict and factionalism.

Clearly, theorists who invoke exit rights are aware of how difficult it is to ensure exit from identity groups.[14] But rarely does this difficulty lead to any skepticism about how we think about the democratic interaction of groups in the first place. To the contrary, the overriding tendency is to pretend that all groups are voluntary associations, that all are trying to advance interests of similar import, and that what is required to protect them all is individual rights.

IV. Conclusion

The comparison here between early and later pluralist ideas might seem to suggest implicitly that the holism and idealism of the earlier pluralists is preferable to the liberal individualism of the post-war pluralists. But this would misread the argument. The approaches of British pluralists to group life, including group-based sovereignty, and the relation between individuals and groups leave many questions unanswered. Nonetheless, these pre-WWII theories were a treasure trove of ideas that did not survive into post-war period. Ideas like the 'moral personality' of groups and corporatism are relevant examples, though ones unlikely to enjoy a renaissance today. A more likely survivor is the awareness, which formed a set of premises in British pluralism, that individual well-being and, in Laski's case, individual liberty, depended on group life, that groups were not primarily or merely instruments to influence state policy, that groups had an important role to play in democratic citizenship, and that group life could be protected by legally protecting groups.

Post-war pluralism gave up on some of these pre-war notions and the result was in some senses a weaker, rather than a stronger, understanding of what individual well-being consists in. Further, the illusion in American democratic theory, for which post-war pluralism is partly responsible, that democracy is constituted by voluntary associations, meant that all the ways in which associations are not voluntary or could not be voluntary were thereby outside of the realm of mainstream democratic politics if not somewhat hostile to the value of democracy. Moreover, the impression advanced, in part, by pluralism's critics, that post-war pluralist theories have little if anything to do with thinking about the role that cultural, religious, or linguistic groups

---

14   Skeptics of the exit option include Weinstock 2005 and Reitman 2005 as well as theorists who focus on children, where the problem of exit (and of liberal notions of autonomy in general) are most apparently and acutely problematic. With respect to children see Reich 2002 and generally, Archard and Macleod eds. (2002).

play in democracy is mistaken. To conceive of all groups as voluntary associations, even when many are not, as the post-war approach did, *is* a way of thinking about and managing groups in democracy and one that continues to obscure many of the questions central to democratic theory about diverse societies today. Earlier pluralists, like Figgis and Laski, certainly did not come up with satisfactory answers to these questions, but in many respects, they had a better grasp of what questions needed to be addressed in order to successfully balance group life and individual freedom in democracy.

Philip G. Cerny

Plurality, Pluralism, and Power: Elements of Pluralist Analysis in an Age of Globalization

The central conceptual conundrum in pluralism involves a tension between two fundamental assumptions: "plurality" as an analytical assumption; and "pluralism" as a predictive and normative assumption.

The plurality assumption, on the one hand, is a statement about inputs. It asserts: (a) that social, economic, and political interaction (including that based on normative values) takes place among people categorized by and/or organized into groups, rather than among atomistic individuals or through reified institutional structures like the state; and (b) that despite significant power differentials among such groups, their fractionalization and the fluidity of their conflict and competition means that power can only be exercised by an ongoing (if uneven) process of coalition-building, rather than through static, embedded power structures.

The pluralism assumption, on the other hand, is a statement about outcomes. It asserts: (a) that the interaction of "organized" and "potential" groups (Truman 1951), "cross-cutting" affiliations (Simmel 1955; Coser 1956) and "overlapping memberships" (Truman 1951), along with the competitive character of liberal democracy, social modernity, and capitalism, together lead to a political system of inherent socio-political checks and balances that prevents monistic forms of domination becoming embedded; and (b) that this condition is normatively desirable, i.e., that a pluralist system is a "good" system (or a "least worst" system) that effectively promotes a quasi-democratic political marketplace of ideas and policies and/or a healthy "civil society" (Eisfeld, this volume).

This chapter argues that the plurality assumption and the pluralism assumption are not only problematic in themselves but also in essential and chronic tension with each other. This tension has become more acute in the era of globalization. These questions have only been unsatisfactorily addressed within the pluralist canon by concepts such as "democratic elitism" and "neopluralism" (e.g., Lindblom 1977). More importantly, however, both assumptions, and the connection between them, are further problematized by their extrapolation to contemporary issues such as commodification and marketization, post-Fordism, consumerism, multiculturalism, postmodernism, the "new security dilemma", state fragmentation and rescaling, transnationalization, globalization, etc. – some of which will be addressed in more detail later in this chapter.

The nearest thing to a pluralist analysis of globalization in recent years has been the revival of the concept of "civil society". However, that concept is both too narrow and too broad to provide an accurate picture of the political sociology of the contemporary world.

On the one hand, in seeking to locate civil society somewhere between, but not fully including, both the market and the state, it focuses on too narrow a range of actors. It can tell us something about, for example, social capital and advocacy coalitions, but not about how political processes work.

On the other hand, it is an inherently normative concept which suggests that the emergence of a global civil society is a good thing mainly because of the sorts of groups it encompasses – i.e., those pursuing more radical and/or solidaristic social agendas (environmentalism, poverty alleviation, etc.) rather than self-interested economic interests (firms, markets) or control-and-stability-oriented political actors (politicians and bureaucrats).

In this chapter I argue that an expanded neopluralist analysis of globalization has significant advantages in terms of understanding not only how globalization itself works in practice but also how globalization in turn reshapes both the configuration of interests and the way inputs are translated into outputs. The result is a complex and conflictual world that, although lacking the homogeneity of a true "civil society", creates possibilities for a fairly broad range of actors at multiple levels and pressure points to influence and manipulate outcomes and to reshape global political processes in significant ways, in both empirical and normative terms.

I. Pluralism as a Contemporary Paradigm

Globalization in analytical terms lies at the crossroads of political science and international relations. Pluralism – especially its near-paradigmatic post-Second World War version – has been on the defensive as an approach to political science since the 1960s, and has never been a major contributor to the development of international relations analysis.

In the first place, as regards political sociology, scholars on both left and right (though mainly the former) have always argued that the maldistribution of resources in society distorts the potential for interests to compete effectively, skewing politics through class, elitism, and/or corporatism. Furthermore, the attention of mainstream political science has increasingly focused on institutions and structures rather than political processes as such, constraining the role that actors – the main empirical focus of pluralist analyses – can play in determining outcomes (Hall and Taylor 1996). Finally, in epistemologically hegemonic realist approaches to international relations, external imperatives deriving from the anarchical character of the international system are said to compel endogenous groups and institutional structures alike to merge into virtual "unit actors" with regard to key issues (Waltz 1979).

This chapter will attempt to go beyond the existing limits of both domestic political science and international relations by reconfiguring both pluralism and globalization – and asserting that the relationship between the two is the central analytical question of the 21st century.

Pluralism, especially in its post-Second World War variant (see chapters by Eisfeld and Eisenberg in this volume), is arguably the most important paradigmatic concept in modern political science, although it is also one of the most contested of such concepts. Unlike the concept of power, traditionally the core of the idea of politics *per se*, it implies that a particular *kind* of configuration of power is at the heart of modern politics; that empirically such pluralist power configurations are for secular reasons becoming more and more hegemonic; and that pluralist politics underlies, and is analytically and temporally prior to, a range of normative as well as empirical considerations such as liberalism, democracy, civil society, human rights, and the like. Unlike ideas such as justice, which underlie forms of political philosophy, pluralism rejects monistic assumptions about how such values may be put into practice; it gives normative primacy to enlightened pragmatism and to the sociological primacy of "groups" (often poorly defined) rather than to categorical values.

This aspect of pluralism sometimes misleads normative political theorists into assuming that the interaction of "groups and interests" that is at the core of pluralist analysis represents merely "the competitive struggle for advantage among private interests and economic utilities", thus "deny[ing] the possibility of arriving at any notion of the common or public good" (Fontana, Nederman, and Remer 2004: 4).

This could not be further from the case. Both radical and conservative pluralists see pluralism as either (or both) empowering popular groups lacking money and control of the means of production potentially to pursue their normative values (as well as their material interests, of course) through normal politics (the radical version), and/or establishing a system of checks and balances that enables a normatively superior consensus to be reached through peaceful competition among those values and interests (the conservative version) (see Eisfeld, this volume).

Finally, unlike structuralism and institutionalism, pluralism gives priority to process and agency – giving the voluntaristic goals of actors ontological as well as epistemological primacy, albeit in the context of bargaining rather than outright conflict or violence – instead of sociological determinism. Pluralism is about real people interacting in the modern (or even postmodern) world in ways that channel power struggles and faction-fighting into negotiation and compromise, smooth the sharp edges of belief into toleration, and engage people in positive-sum coalition-building activities that will not merely lead to stability but – one hopes – to cooperative, positive-sum, "win-win", or at least Pareto-efficient, welfare outcomes. It is a statement about how complex social reality can give rise to ongoing mutual adjustment – and, indeed, the emergence of a pragmatically arrived-at public or common good – rather than to the fragmentation, stalemate, institutional bias, and/or negative-sum outcomes associated with theories of power, domination, and hegemony.

Nevertheless, the very discursive power of the pluralist paradigm is also its greatest weakness. Pluralism can alternatively be seen as overstated, over-determined, and giving rise to a bland, polyanna-ish misconstruction of what is really going on in political life.

To see pluralism everywhere, first of all, is to miss the real, underlying power struggles that determine "who gets what, when, and how" (Lasswell 1950). Furthermore, the apparent hegemony of pluralism may be first and foremost a mask for a particular embedded structure of power, especially that of capitalism. As Lenin said, "Democracy is the best shell for capitalism", and much has been made of pluralism as mirroring the surface level of competing capitals while the power relations of the capitalism system as a whole not only remain unaltered but also determine the most significant outcomes of political processes.

Pluralism may also fundamentally misconstrue the struggle discussed above over normative beliefs and values. When those beliefs, as they often do, form around competing interpretations of metaphysical truth, compromise and toleration may simply represent temporary and unstable balances of power just waiting to be challenged in the name of higher certainties. Twenty-first-century religious fundamentalism, like mid-20th century political ideologies before it, is a case in point.

Finally, the basic categories of pluralist analysis – individuals categorized and/or organized into groups – may simply confuse dependent and independent variables. In Marxist analysis, of course, the apparent or surface-level politics of groups is a form of false consciousness that misses the underlying structural homologies of class, whereas for Weberians and institutionalists those groups simply coagulate around structured points of access and control.

The consequence of the interaction of these trends has been that scholarly debates about globalization have tended to focus on independent variables rooted in structural change – or continuities. These debates concern such phenomena as the significance of economic globalization in bringing about political change, the domestic "hollowing out" (or not) of the state, and/or whether the development of complex interdependence, international regimes, global governance and the like are altering the fundamental character of in-ternational – and transnational – relations.

What is not always clear in this context is what sort of capacity and scope individual and group actors may possess to determine outcomes and, indeed, to shape the sociological, institutional and international contexts in which they operate. I have argued elsewhere that it is possible to construct a range of hypotheses about the roles and potential scope for political action of different types of actors in the context of globalization using a structurational approach (Cerny 2000a). (The term "structuration" in social science theory was first used by Piaget and has been developed in particular by Anthony Giddens [1979].) I have also applied neopluralist theory to globalization in a somewhat different way than in this chapter (Cerny 2003a). Here I will expand this analysis by constructing further hypotheses about how globalization and pluralization interact dynamically, altering the character of political processes in a globalizing world.

In doing so I will distinguish my notion of a pluralist – or neopluralist – approach from what I take to be the closest approximation to a pluralist analysis of globalization in current political science and international relations, i.e. the notion of "global civil society".

Of course, this concept can be defined in a way that is quite like some traditional pluralist analyses. It focuses on the role of interest and pressure groups and sees these as developing an autonomous political capacity to organize and operate transnationally, affecting the issues highlighted earlier – the distribution of resources, the degree of interlock between groups and the state, the structure of institutional constraints and opportunities, and the development of new political and institutional strategies and tactics to cope with interdependence and international system change.

In the development of this analysis, structural and institutional factors, such as path dependency and change, will be treated not as fully-fledged independent variables. Rather they will be seen as a mix of dependent, independent, and facilitating variables that constitute so-called "choice points" or "multiple equilibria": relatively constraining and/or permissive conditions within which actors operate and which they can also manipulate and, to a greater or lesser degree, reshape (Cerny 2000a).

II. Pluralism and Modernity

Pluralism is, first and foremost, an approach to modernity. In particular, pluralism stands in opposition to explanations of modernity couched in the language of gigantism – whether the all-seeing Panoptikon bureaucratic state (Burchell, Gordon and Miller 1991; Weber 1947), the submergence of people in increasingly larger (and fewer) socio-economic classes (the Marxist tradition), the collaboration of corporatist or neocorporatist "peak associations" (Schmitter 1974), or the all-encompassing "nation".

In contrast, pluralism is rooted in the notion that a complex array of individuals and groups operates within multi-level state – and other institutional –

structures with "multiple points of access" (Truman 1951). Such groups include "overlapping" (Truman 1951) and "cross-cutting" groups, (Simmel 1955; Coser 1956), socio-economic "sectional" and value-based "cause" groups. These groups are inherently involved in a process of fungible coalition-building that is always at least to some extent in flux ("a great moving process": Bentley 1908) and they bring together multiple loyalties and identities.

While the need to reconcile these differences among groups at one level appears to make the nation-state a necessary but not sufficient condition for compromise and political progress (Cerny 1999a), at the same time such differences contain within them the potential to problematize both the nation and the state. At the same time, unlike purely individualistic interpretations of modernity, pluralist modernity suggests that individuals will not become anomic, alienated beings, nor will they spontaneously act out rationalistic games with each other; rather, they will find both identity and choice rooted in their underlying social plurality, their multiple group memberships.

In this context, the plurality assumption – which is the main positivistic, analytical root of pluralism – has been seen to be inextricably intertwined with the normative assertion that pluralism is a good thing. In this context, nations are not organic units of which people are subsidiary members. Rather they are cumulative, pragmatic, conventional expressions of multiple coalition-building processes. Those coalitions form, break up and re-form, providing a repertoire of choices that is asserted to be greater than that which is available through simple territorial representation. Classes, elites, and corps neither dominate perpetually nor struggle holistically, but are themselves riven by cleavages that permit more complex coalitions form around more specific shared interests and value goals. And the best form of government is assumed to be characterized – like the system of separation of powers and federalism in the United States (especially for Truman 1951) – by institutions that provide multiple points of access and checks and balances, to ensure that politics, like a well-functioning political marketplace, will eventually produce a more efficient allocation of resources and values (Easton 1953) than would be possible where more rigid hierarchies rule by fiat – or, indeed, where anomic individuals become alienated and abdicate their already marginalized sovereignty to those hierarchies.

A pluralist version of modernity therefore provides stability by replacing class conflict with stabilizing, cross-cutting conflicts; gives real or virtual representation to the greatest possible number; provides an institutional bulwark against monism; and rewards those actors who choose enlightened self-interest over predatory or monopolistic politics. Pluralist theory also exists in ongoing interaction with the development of modern society – positing that industrial society actually *multiplies* underlying socio-economic "interests", rather than shoehorning them into classes, while the development of mass culture, rather than indoctrinating people into macro-level "groupthink" (Orwell 1949), actually provides a growing repertoire of competing ideas and values that civilize and expand people's horizons. The latter is, of course, a hugely controversial notion in the debate over the increasing corporatization (and "dumbing down?") of the mass media.

The critical problem with this vision, of course, is that the normative outcome – pluralism as an "-ism" – does not necessarily arise from plurality. Indeed, traditional concepts not only of class but more directly of "faction" suggest that plurality will normally lead to *increased* conflict and disorder if not somehow counteracted by other structural and political constraints. Competing interests would lead not to consensus but to endemic power struggles – anarchy instead of accommodation.

A number of both critics of and apologists for pluralism (e.g., Michels 1962, on the one hand, and Rose 1967, on the other) have argued that interest groups are themselves inherently undemocratic and monistic in their endogenous structure, because even when a group starts out as a democratic association, the necessities of managing that group and competing with other groups means that strategic and even tactical control, including financial control, is increasingly ceded to elites *within* the group. Therefore the interaction of those groups with others – their exogenous activities as distinct from their endogenous processes – will ultimately be determined to a large extent, perhaps even hegemonically, by the self-interests of the groups' leaders, especially their interests in organizational and personal survival and maintaining their own status – something they have in common with the leaders of other groups. In such a case, mutual accommodation and bargaining would lead to oligopoly and cartel-like behavior rather than democratic or liberal pluralism. Furthermore, "group politics" might well be likely to lead to greater inequality among groups; many goals, including economic goals but also "positional" goals (Hirsch 1976) are in essence zero-sum in nature, so that when one group wins, another loses.

Individuals, as has been pointed out incessantly in collective action and rational choice theory (Olson 1965), will often "free ride" on the activities of groups. This makes the group's action less effective and, paradoxically, potentially both more conflictual and more hierarchical. Indeed, the very fact of multiple or overlapping group membership may undermine the capacity of individuals to act in a coherent participatory manner; conflict among their various identities, loyalties and values creates an inner conflictedness that can once again lead to alienation and openness to conflictual behavior (Haugaard 2003), especially in a privatized world of eroding social capital (Putnam 2000). Groups, rather than acting in pluralistic fashion, may on the contrary act in monopolistic or oligopolistic fashion to entrench their influence and power – indeed, as they have always done. What looks like open pluralism may, on the contrary, be a form of closed corporatism, whereby "iron trian-

gles" and relationships of "capture", "patronage", and "clientelism" in effect
make groups part of the ruling bureaucracy and *vice-versa* (Streeck and
Schmitter 1986).

Even without a division of society into Marx's form of class structure,
some groups simply possess far more relevant resources of various kinds than
others and are likely to control outcomes because of their "privileged positions"
(Lindblom 1977). And, of course, political and economic institutions, whatever their internal structure, are always inherently biased in that they provide
greater access to some claimants than others.

Therefore pluralism seems less like a spontaneous, bottom-up process
in which the existence of plurality as such produces the desired normative
outcomes in some linear or predetermined fashion, but instead one in which
plural*ism* must be *manufactured* through the transformation of plurality into
pluralistic practices by other means. Structural and institutional factors are
crucial facilitating variables in this process. In analogous fashion to the way
neo-Marxist theorists such as Nicos Poulantzas and Bob Jessop argue that the
capitalist state is not produced automatically by economic or material factors
but is rooted in "extra-economic coercion" (Jessop 2002), so pluralism must
be channeled through, and may even be seen to be generated by, structural
and institutional frameworks that enable, sustain, and reinforce pluralist practices – extra-group support structures.

In other words, for plurality to be transformed into pluralism, it is necessary for there to be a *pluralism-generating and pluralism-reinforcing playing
field* in existence (or at least under construction) that maximizes (or at least
supports) the possibilities for groups to associate, to construct identities that
legitimate and internalize pluralistic practices, to develop strategies and tactics around bargaining and coalition-building rather than conflict and violence, and to be able effectively to influence socio-economic and political
outcomes in significant ways.

The existence of pluralism as distinct from mere plurality, then, requires
the presence of two conditions.

The first is that there must be in one form or another a genuine plurality
of socio-political and/or socio-economic forces in society at large – at whatever level, from the local to the global, and not just at the level of the nation-
state – whether extant or potential, organized or spontaneous, manifest or
latent.

The second is that a supportive context for pluralism – in terms of both
the structural/institutional environment *and* the practices of relevant actors –
must be in place or in the process of being created. Whether a plurality of
forces is present can therefore be the result of either the existence of an already functioning plural socio-political structure *or* the possibility of *creating
or generating* such a structure through proactive politics, especially by what
have been called "political (or institutional) entrepreneurs". Pluralism there-

fore is *mutually constituted* through the interaction of an existing (or constructed) plurality of social forces, on the one hand, and the presence (or construction) of a pluralism-generating playing field, on the other.

The key to this process of mutual constitution is the role of individual and group *actors* in intervening, managing, manipulating, reshaping, and reconstructing both plurality and pluralism. Thus plural*ism* is what *actors* make of it. In this sense, of course, pluralism will only be constructed when actors act in a pluralizing or pluralism-supporting fashion; it can be blocked, constrained, and/or eroded *either* by hierarchically-oriented actors (authoritarian politicians, high-handed bureaucrats, monopolistic or oligopolistic economic actors, patriarchical social elites, monistic religious leaders, etc.) *or* by defecting individuals and groups that act through conflict, violence, or exit rather than through bargaining and compromise. Pluralistic political processes require the capacity not only to counteract such actors (and their structural/institutional resources) but also to generate and maintain alternative, more pluralistic structures and practices.

In effect, pluralism must be supported by what Foucault has called "governmentality", which he defines as the capacity and will of key actors reflexively and proactively to reconcile, in an ongoing and ever-evolving fashion, the core paradox of modernity – i.e., the tension between its Saint-Simonian administrative (or "police") dimension, on the one hand, and its liberalizing, individualizing, and pluralizing dimension, on the other (Burchell, Gordon, and Miller 1991; Cerny 2003b).

Thus, for example, the state – especially a kind of pluralistic, liberal-democratic national state, with most politicians and bureaucrats either dedicated to or enmeshed in the practices of governmentality – has often been seen to be *functionally necessary* to the development of pluralism itself. Such a national state constitutes a playing field that brings conflicting factions into some sort of stable coexistence, even mixing pluralism with supporting organizational props that may not be pluralistic in and of themselves, but which paradoxically contribute to stabilizing, functioning, and maintaining pluralist processes. Classic examples include the sort of top-down coercion, including varieties of absolutism, that undermined feudal structures in 17th century Europe, the institutionalization of formally differentiated, command-style bureaucratic hierarchies (Weber 1947), various quasi-spontaneous hierarchy-producing organizational processes (Michels 1962: "Who says organization says oligarchy"), the continuing and sometimes renewed influence of status-based social hierarchies or authority structures (Eckstein 1965; Huntington 1968; Mayer 1981), or a combination of these.

David Truman (1951), one of the main post-war theorists of the pluralist paradigm, includes much that is virtually institution-centered in his analysis. However, rather than emphasizing the organizational aspects of these institutions, he focuses on their pluralism-supporting and pluralism-generating aspects – especially his emphasis on the multiple points of access characteristic of the American system of government.

Similarly, nations as such can be seen to be artificial political-cultural creations intended to inculcate, through a sense of belonging, an identity with a particular form of common good or public interest that would transcend faction (Anderson 1983). Indeed, democratic or quasi-democratic forms of nationalism would be crucial for channeling factions into pluralistic behavior. Socio-political elites, whether ruling monistically through a pyramid-like structure, or competing with each other for popular votes (Schumpeter 1942), would in effect impose order while indirectly supporting a limited pluralism ("democratic elitism"). Political parties would "aggregate interests" in order to create a kind of artificial, manipulated pluralism through "polyarchy" (Dahl 1972; Duverger 1951). Norms handed down through "political culture" would socialize people into thinking pluralistically (Almond and Verba 1965).

And, of course, liberal – pluralistic – democracy could still be seen as "the best shell for capitalism", assuming of course that it was a relatively compctititive – non-monopolistic – form of capitalism, ruled by Adam Smith's "invisible hand" – i.e., a kind of market capitalism that could in theory both prevent capitalists from coalescing to permanently dominate the system and allow non-business groups to exert significant influence in shaping outcomes. In advocating a "neopluralist" approach, Lindblom (1977) argues that despite the "privileged position of business", the scope for pluralism is still significant in contemporary capitalist societies.

III. Pluralism as a Political Project

All in all, then, an understanding of how plurality and pluralism are related in the real world, and not just the world of traditional pluralist theory, requires an understanding of how all of these factors are managed and manipulated by political actors – especially those more influential actors often called "political entrepreneurs" or "institutional entrepreneurs" – into moving towards a more normatively desirable form of pluralistic stabilization, mutual adjustment, liberal democratization and representation (territorial *and* virtual), the protections of a functioning and open legal system, civil rights, free and competitive elections, fairly widespread participation, informational transparency, and an acceptance of common norms of civility, compromise and consensus-building. Such a process, as argued above, is rooted in the mutual constitution of plurality and a pluralism-supporting playing field.

In fact, none of these goals are ever achieved once and for all, and there is no pure pluralism found anywhere in the world. Pluralism, like all political projects, has to be imagined and constructed by means of a normative political project that is always contested. This contestation takes two main forms.

In the first place, pluralism is contested internally. There are always conflicts, whether rooted in inequalities or clashing values. These include old conflicts that are embedded or entrenched, not only in society and the economy, but also in the relationship among various institutions, agencies, and levels of the state. As governments have become increasingly involved in redistributive and regulatory activities over the past century and a half, there have always been winners and losers. Within the state, competing priorities are never fully reconciled – whether social spending *versus* defense spending, poverty reduction *versus* support for growth-producing business elites, finance ministries *versus* "spending ministries", etc. Within society, old inequalities persist and new ones develop.

Secondly, pluralism is contested externally. New claimants continually arise, especially through globalization and the transnationalization of group linkages, whether among businesses – especially multinational corporations, but also including any businesses and workers affected by restructuring, downsizing, outsourcing, reskilling/deskilling, and/or the search for export markets to replace lost domestic markets – consumer interests, diasporas, environmental or other cause groups, religious and ethnic communities, transgovernmental networks (Slaughter 2004), AIDS sufferers, tsunami victims, or terrorists (Cerny 2005).

Resolving these conflicts does not come easily. Nevertheless, key elites and groups, in trial and error fashion, have throughout modernity sought to develop what sociologists call reflexive "practices" that revolve around the continuing and ever-evolving necessities of achieving such resolution(s) on a day-to-day as well as on a long-term basis.

IV. Pluralism and Globalization: The Disaggregation of the Political Process

In a globalizing world, the tools of manipulation and conflict management are far more complex and problematic than within the traditional playing field (partly materially real, partly imagined or even mythical) of the nation-state.

In the first place, the state, once part of the solution, is increasingly seen to be part of the problem, whether in terms of its organizational and institutional structures and processes, its character as an arena of collective action, or its capacity to constitute a "unitary actor" and make "credible commitments" in international affairs. Globalization has increasingly "problematized" the state itself, undermining it in some ways, transforming it in others, and reinforcing it in yet others (Cerny 1999b).

Secondly, the nation and the notion of national identity are increasingly problematized too. Whether through cultural heterogeneity and fragmentation – McLuhan's "global village" often looks like a "global jungle" – consumerism or civil wars, the focus of a basic sense of belonging on the nation and the nation-state is slipping away, despite attempts to resurrect and reinforce it.

Thirdly, economic policy and policymaking are increasingly constrained and homogenized by the need not just for states but for businesses to compete in the global marketplace, even if that process of convergence produces its own old and new inequalities and divergences.

Finally, the process of group politics is increasingly complicated by the emergence of a complex, multilayered set of new groups – often called, or confused with, non-governmental organizations (NGOs) – that are characterized by all the same ambiguities and distortions that have been found in national-level pressure groups, but without the same kinds of constraints. Meanwhile, political parties, corporatist structures, and other national-level "intermediaries" (to use de Tocqueville's term: de Tocqueville 1955), are increasingly at a loss to cope with the challenges of the disaggregation of the political process that comes with globalization. Actors and groups are thus enmeshed in a long-term learning process.

The state, firstly, is still there – it is not disappearing, but it is disaggregating. It has long been a key element of pluralist analysis that the existence of multiple points of access to the political process is a fundamental part of the way plurality is stabilized and channeled into "pluralism". But in a globalizing world, the further multiplication of points of access – both their verticalization into international organizations, regimes, and other dimensions of "global governance", on the one hand, and their transnational horizontal expansion across borders – comes without the organizational constraints that a centripetal set of domestic state institutions possesses. Eckstein's and Huntington's notion that the maintenance of underlying non-democratic social authority structures is required for democratic stability (Eckstein 1965; Huntington 1968) not only does not work in a globalizing world – authority structures are too fragmented and hegemony too is a fragile reed (Cerny 2006) – but attempts to impose authority in a still quasi-anarchic international order can exacerbate conflict and be self-defeating.

In this context, groups have to organize in ways that demand both flexibilization and stronger elite leadership. The emerging concept of "multi-level governance" represents a structurally open and problematic playing field; indeed, it is probably better conceived as complex, *multi-nodal politics* (Cerny, forthcoming). Of course, to use Lindblom's term, the privileged position of business is dramatically increased, as multinational corporations and international financial markets possess the lion's share of the kind of resources necessary to pursue their interests on this complex playing field. But in a more open, globalizing world, it is harder for multinational corporations to be economically or organizationally monopolistic, as there are more competitors out there from different points of the compass, including from increasingly vibrant emerging markets. Only in certain product areas, like commercial aircraft, are economies of scale and transactions costs so large that only one or two producers can corner the global market and act oligopolistically.

States, too, as Slaughter (2004) has demonstrated, have lost much of their endogenous policymaking coherence as transgovernmental networks of regulators, lawyers and judges, and even legislators form the backbone of an informal but increasingly dense process of indirect global governance. The politics of redistribution is everywhere being replaced by the "beanbag" politics of regulation, as regulations – often adopted in the name of so-called "deregulation" – proliferate and become ever more all-encompassing and hierarchical (Moran 2003; Levi-Faur and Jordana 2005). The more you punch the beanbag, the more it just absorbs the punishment and mutates into new shapes. In this world, although political parties and foreign policymakers still pretend that the state constitutes a sovereign arena of collective action, it is increasingly drawn into transnational webs of governance (Cerny 2002).

Paradoxically, democratization too means absorption into this world of pooled (and lost) sovereignty, regulatory diffusion, marketization, and the hegemony of neoliberalism. And at the level of foreign policymaking, even the United States under the current George W. Bush administration, keen to demonstrate its autonomy and hegemonic leadership, is increasingly pulled into the quagmire of imperial overstretch (Cerny 2006). Global governance or the "new international architecture" or "public sphere" simply does not have either the coercive power or the organizational coherence to promote and stabilize plurality and transform it into pluralism – yet.

In this world, secondly, alternative points of identity are crowding out national identity. Nation-states rarely go to war with each other, but civil and cross-border wars, tribalism and ethnic conflicts, and other new forms of international violence like terrorism are proliferating. Push them down in one place and they pop up in another. Transnational diasporas are increasingly significant as the internet and other forms of long-distance communication and information transfer allow migrant groups to maintain contacts in ways that were far more difficult (although still significant) in the past (Yuval-Davis 2000; Nordstrom 2000).

In economic terms, the common identity that in the "modern" nation-state (i.e., from the mid-19th to the mid-20th centuries) derived from producer interests that linked Second Industrial Revolution enterprises with national industrialization, the rise of trade unions, and the welfare state, is being increasingly swamped by transnational markets, post-Fordism, and fickle consumer interests (Cerny 1995). These interests care only about buying the cheapest goods available on the world market.

This is not to belittle consumerism, because it has enabled many groups previously subsumed into class and caste identities to improve their standard of living and to exercise an important if problematic form of "choice". But consumerism, and indeed marketization itself, are essentially a-national and diffuse, undermining collective solidarities as industries themselves flexibilize in post-Fordist fashion and lose their national identities; the globalization of financial markets has been a key driver of this process (Cerny 1993). A true McDonaldization of world culture may be a long way away and consumer tastes can be highly diverse, but that does not mean that they can generate the kind of social capital once believed to be at the heart of domestic social solidarity and identity within a relatively insulated national economy. Lifestyles of all classes are globalizing, but in ways that augment plurality while potentially undermining pluralism.

Thirdly, as has been so often observed, economic policy and policymaking are increasingly being shaped by international and transnational factors. Macroeconomic policy is constrained by global flows of trade and finance. Domestic social policy is converging around the streamlining and marketizing of welfare states. Trade and industrial policies are concerned primarily with the competitive position of domestically based economic activities in international marketplaces – the shift of emphasis from the welfare state to the "competition state" (Cerny 1990, 1997, 2000b). And regulatory policies, noted above, are increasingly focused on pro-market re-regulation rather than deregulation or decommodification (Levi-Faur and Jordana 2005). Such shifts do allow for – and even necessitate – domestic variation, which creates some scope for groups of winners and losers from globalization to organize (Lütz 2004; Soederberg, Menz, and Cerny 2002). However, the technocratic imperatives of adapting to globalization increasingly take priority over redistributive and welfare goals.

Fourthly, of course, new groups are emerging and exerting pressure at international and transnational levels. Indeed, the proliferation of NGOs, whether business organizations, environmental groups, broad social movements, or pressure groups in specific issue-areas, must focus not only on national governments but also on coordinating a range of pressure-type activities from the local to the global levels.

Some international regimes, like the United Nations, have been very active in attempting to co-opt such groups into more formalized arenas of consultation on a whole range of issues and decisionmaking processes, while others have tried to keep them at arm's length. Some international regimes have indeed been "captured" by such groups, and *vice-versa*.

These groups, as noted above, also exhibit the same internal organizational tendencies to elite hierarchy as traditional pressure groups and are conflicted as to whether to become virtual parts of the growing bureaucracy of global governance or to maintain their outsider status. At the same time, they must both cooperate and conflict with other groups in overlapping issue-areas, forming alliances and coalitions across borders. Activist groups in issue-areas like the environment, for example, must coordinate local activism, pressure on local and sub-national regional governmental structures, national governments and international regimes, with media and other communications activities at all levels, as well as interacting with other interest and pressure groups both locally and in other parts of the world (Betsill 1999; Cerny 2000a).

The requirements of influence are highly complex and require not only a high degree of flexibilization but an increasingly proactive role on the part of political and institutional entrepreneurs to create new arenas and networks to coordinate that influence. At the peak, business and governmental groups come together in arenas like the World Economic Forum with its annual meetings in Davos, Switzerland, where business leaders and political decisionmakers debate global issues, while social-sectional and cause groups increasingly attempt to provide an alternative focus through the World Social Forum that until recently has been meeting annually in Puerto Alegre, Brazil. Political leaders of the center-left, such as President Luis Inaçio Lula da Silva of Brazil, attempt to bridge both sorts of meetings.

V. Pluralism and the Limits of Global Civil Society

In this wider, multi-level and multi-nodal world, the relationship between plurality and pluralism becomes more and more complex and problematic. The privileged position of business interests is of course augmented by their control of financial resources, information, managerial skills, network complementarities deriving from the globalization of trade, production, financial and information flows, and other advantages.

At the same time, "resistance" to globalization, as expressed in the demonstrations against the World Trade Organization in Seattle in 1999, are giving way to more complex, globally-oriented networks, strategies and tactics among cause and social-sectional groups. These developments have given rise to the concept that pluralism is simply reorganizing itself at transnational level into a phenomenon called "global civil society" (Edwards 2004).

However, the notion of global civil society is both too narrow and too broad to provide an accurate picture of the changing political sociology of the contemporary world. On the one hand, in seeking to locate civil society somewhere between, but not fully including, both the market and the state, the global civil society literature focuses on too narrow a range of actors. Of course, the concept of civil society itself is notoriously fungible and in the history of political thought it has been defined sometimes to include, sometimes to exclude, both economic processes like markets and political structures like the state (Ehrenberg 1999; Fontana 2006).

Civil society is usually defined to *exclude* both of these, to identify a middle ground, rooted in political culture, normative values and social interaction, that constitutes and independent variable alongside markets and states – a kind of third force in the globalization process. Thus it can tell us something about, for example, social capital and advocacy coalitions, and how they organize people and influence political outcomes, but in this context both the economy and the state are exogenous to civil society itself. I argue that this does not tell us very much about how political processes actually work, as it underestimates the extent to which individual and group actors are themselves embedded in economic and political-institutional contexts. Civil society is too narrow a concept to comprehend the politics of globalization.

On the other hand, in the history of political thought civil society is and always been an inherently normative concept which, extended to present-day issues, suggests that the emergence of a global civil society is a good thing. In contrast to the self-interest of economic actors and the institutional vested interests of politicians and bureaucrats, civil society is often seen as aiming higher and infusing globalization with the kind of values that can create a new normative order in a changing world (Ehrenberg 1999). This potential for positive normative outcomes derives mainly from the sorts of groups civil society is said to encompass – i.e., those pursuing more solidaristic cross-border social agendas such as environmentalism and ecology, poverty alleviation, improving the position of women, aiding politically oppressed groups, opposing inequalities on a world scale rather than just within one country, and the like (Keck and Sikkink 1998).

These are essentially what traditional pluralist analysis called "cause groups", as distinct from "sectional groups". They are said to have an increasing capacity, although always problematic, to "think globally" but "act locally", to possess a sort of "variable geometry" that allows them to operate tactically and strategically on a range of different institutional planes and through differentiated political processes, and to create new agendas that would normally be precluded by the operation of economic interests and embedded political-institutional structures and processes. In this sense they are *strategically located* within global society in ways that reinforce their capacity to shape change (Cerny 2000a).

At the same time, however, the very attractiveness of the concept of global civil society limits its usefulness as an analytical framework. For all the potential of global civil society, it is to a large extent an analytical mirage. For its very emergence, and the political and economic processes the groups that make it up operate within, are also the product of more general political and economic changes that have created not only these groups but a much broader pluralization of global politics. To look at the attainments of global civil society does highlight some real achievements, but it also draws a veil over what I believe to be even more important dimensions of pluralization.

In this analysis I am to some extent critiquing my own earlier work. Although I have asserted previously that what I identified in highly schematized form as "social actors" may have greater potential to shape the future order of a globalizing world than "economic actors" and/or "political actors" (Cerny 2000a, 2003a) – arguing that social actors are more likely to take an increasingly proactive or "transformative" approach to political action, while economic and political actors in the narrow sense are more likely to be "reactive" or "adaptive" – I now believe that the impact of social actors is somewhat more limited because of the very fact that they do not sufficiently penetrate economic structures and political processes across the board. Indeed, most of the concrete changes in the way actors influence political processes and outcomes do tend to stem from the more indirect impact of changes in habits and patterns of action by reactive/adaptive (political and economic) actors and not just from the more direct impact of proactive/transformative ones.

Therefore it is crucial to identify those more indirect influences by looking at (a) the redistribution of resources and the organizational restructuring of the socio-economic base, (b) the changing ways different groups interact and interlock with states and other state-like institutional structures, and (c) the restructuring of the playing field itself. This chapter argues that at all three levels it is possible to identify a broad but uneven pluralization of world politics, whether at the level of what one might call the "raw material" of those political processes in terms of individual and group actors and the Bentleyan "interests" they reflect and represent or in the way those interests are reshaped in the translation or transformation of raw inputs into those political processes that in turn shape outcomes. In this sense, it is the mutual, reciprocal interaction of actors and structures that is at the core of the analysis.

However, what is important is not structural change in and of itself, nor just how that change involves new sets of constraints and opportunities for actors, but, again, what actors do with those constraints and opportunities. Institutional change is at one level a set of constraints, but at another level a process which enables and empowers actors to re-conceive what they are doing and wish to do, and indeed to re-conceive what their interests really are in a changing world.

Actors do not operate on a *tabula rasa* or make history in conditions of their own choosing, but globalization, I argue, actually *opens up new spaces for action more than it closes them down*. Globalization, while not yet a finished pluralist construct, increasingly involves a set of "permissive conditions" for change, not just for civil society actors but for a much larger set or sets of actors. Whereas "modern" (i.e., 17th–20th century) national culture societies, national political systems, and "inter-national" relations restricted most actors, except for state actors (diplomats) and certain international businesspeople, to the domestic stage, globalization pulls more and more actors outwards, downwards, and upwards, both forcing and drawing them in to operate on, and to attempt to manipulate and reshape, a complex mix of old and new international, transnational, regional, translocal, and local stages and playing fields. Given the range of alternative "multiple equilibria" that are becoming available for actors to aim at across these different stages, globalization is increasingly what actors make of it.

Therefore globalization *is* pluralism in the making – or at least a kind of uneven pluralization – but in a more thoroughgoing, less bounded sense than traditional national-level pluralism. A globalizing world is a pluralizing world.

However, that pluralism is not the ideal-type, fractionalized (see below), self-regulating, self-stabilizing pluralism of mid-20th-century American pluralist political theorists. It is not the political equivalent of (relatively) perfect competition – or, as today's economists would have it, of portfolio diversification with its balancing of speculation and hedging. It can be dis-equilibrating and destabilizing, rooted in unequal distributions of resources, locked in through restructured socio-political hierarchies and changing coalitions, and filtered through increasingly complex institutional webs reaching above, below and through the state.

At first glance it looks more like what Dahl and Lindblom called "neo-pluralism", but it lacks the embeddedness and hierarchical simplicity of that sort of structure; it is in flux. Therefore what actors do – how they pursue their interests and values, how they organize themselves, how they determine political outcomes, and how they reshape the institutional superstructure – will become more and more important in the future. What *kind* of pluralization emerges will determine what sort of world order crystallizes out of that flux.

In looking at these issues, I will first address the question of how pluralism can be developed as an analytical framework in the context of globalization. I will then examine globalization itself, focusing on its character as a set of permissive conditions in which actors' opportunities are expanded, however unevenly. And finally I will look at how the interaction of globalization and pluralization leads to a messy but increasingly pluralized but uneven and shifting world order with complex new levels and spaces – but one which is likely to be shaped over time through practices developed by actors themselves in the process of pluralization through a combination of trial-and-error plus increasingly strategic rationalization.

VI. Globalization and Pluralization: A Multi-Level Approach

The processes of globalization and pluralization are inextricably intertwined. Actors of various kinds – whether political entrepreneurs, reactive/adaptive state and economic actors, interest groups (both "sectional" and "cause" or value groups), or even "masses" – are not only constrained but also empowered in several ways by both path dependency and by long-term structural changes.

In this ever-evolving context, such actors act strategically not simply to pursue their material interests and normative values, but even more significantly to shape and reshape the emerging politics of a globalizing world in complex ways. Hendrik Spruyt refers to "institutional selection" (Spruyt 1994), although that term is too limited, as it does not in itself focus enough attention on the shaping of political processes and practices as well as more formal institutions. Bob Jessop calls this aspect of political life "strategic selectivity", a term that is perhaps more apt in the context of this chapter (Jessop 2002). The strategies and tactics adopted by actors to cope with, control (including damage control), manage, and restructure political institutions, processes, and practices that determine what sort of globalization we get.

Spruyt, in his perceptive analysis of the transition from feudalism to the nation-state, develops an extremely useful three-stage model to analyze such broad patterns of historical change. A revised version of this model lies behind the analysis here.

The first stage involves the emergence and consolidation of certain political, social, and material preconditions for transition, which he calls "exogenous independent variables". In the case of the transition from feudalism to the nation-state in Europe, those conditions consisted mainly of various underlying social and economic changes, in particular the emergence of what he calls "translocal trade". In other words, a combination of technological developments that enabled early manufacture to grow, plus innovations in transportation and communication, plus the emergence of new classes of merchants and producers to compete with the feudal aristocracy, plus an explosion of new consumer demands in swelling late medieval cities, etc., transformed the socio-economic environment within which political institutions, processes, and practices functioned. Some old groups declined in wealth, prestige, and political clout, while others were able to profit from these changes by altering their own practices; at the same time, some new groups – especially new merchants and manufacturers – drove the processes of change while others, like the urban poor, lost out.

The second stage involves the "restructuring of socio-political coalitions", i.e. a changing cosmos of political allegiances and alliances vying to get a grip on change and reorient policy outcomes accordingly. Developments such as standing armies, navies, new financial systems, trade promotion and protection, taxation, bureaucratization, etc. – including deep conflicts over such changes, as in the English Civil War and later the French Revolution – were part and parcel of this process. For example, some parts of the aristocracy became isolated in their agricultural fastnesses while others linked up with rising financial and commercial elites and converted their old resources into new, profit-making activities – re-entrenching their political power through absolutism.

In the third stage, these tactics of conversion began to be transformed into broader structural strategies not so much for simply managing change and controlling power as for constructing the future through establishing new political institutions, developing new political processes, and embedding new political practices. These strategies were not just about reacting to change but also *capturing the benefits of those changes* in the longer term, whether for personal or group advantage, or for the direct or indirect advantage of the society as a whole – e.g., political stabilization, economic growth, or social development.

Clearly this was a process with plurality, and a certain amount of proto-pluralism, at its heart, characterized by complex changing patterns of conflict, competition, and coalition-building among an evolving (and sometimes rapidly changing) cast of group characters. Eventually, after a couple of false starts (the Venetian city-state and the Hanseatic League), the 16th-century French nation-state emerged as the dominant "arena of collective action" or playing field for uneven political processes and reinforced its structural dominance through the emergence of an international "states system" based on the mutual acceptance of the legitimacy and autonomy of other, similar states (the capacity of states to make "credible commitments") (Spruyt 1994).

In adapting this model and applying it to the relationship between globalization and pluralization, we are therefore concerned primarily with *three* overlapping and linked levels of analysis – not the two levels, "inside" and "outside", that have previously characterized the division of political and academic labor between political science and international relations. These reflect an old, Tocquevillean tradition in political sociology, between the base, intermediaries, and the superstructure and political processes characteristic of the political system – not in this case, however, confined to national political systems, but involving a complex, multilayered, and multi-nodal global political system.

Although this analytical schema at first glance appears synchronic, as distinct from the historical analysis of Spruyt, in fact these three levels link well with his three stages, which indeed are not chronologically distinct stages in any case but rather a mixture of synchronic and asynchronic processes. Globalization as a political process involves the interaction of actors functioning at – and across – all three of these levels.

The first, the base, concerns such factors as: the distribution of resources in society; the kind of processes of production, distribution and exchange prevalent therein; the state of consciousness or the perception of interests, values and possibilities of the various individual and group actors; and the sorts of basic solidarities and alliances of a more political nature that emerge from the first three.

The second concerns what de Tocqueville called the character of "intermediaries", or the openness or closure of political processes and coalitions that transform the raw material of the base into more specific political and economic resources within a narrower political process – sometimes called the power structure. How open or closed are elites? Is there a coherent, instrumental "ruling class", or a more nebulous Gramscian "hegemonic bloc" (Fontana 1993 and 2006)? Do interests interact systematically with politicians, bureaucrats, etc., in a corporatist or neo-corporatist fashion? What embedded alliances have evolved over time, and how open or flexible are they? Is public policy made by iron triangles, closed policy communities, wider policy networks, or transparent, competitive, quasi-democratic processes?

And the third concerns the structure of the institutional playing fields themselves, whether concentrated or diffused, unitary or fragmented, and the sorts of rules and practices that have evolved to coordinate different levels and/or pillars of the political system.

A. The Base

The key to understanding the role of the base (plurality) in enabling the construction of pluralism as such is to understand the distinction between simple *plurality*, on the one hand, and *fractionalization*, on the other. There are qualitatively and quantitatively different configurations of plurality.

The first concerns the number of significant group actors in any political system. Elitist, class-based and corporatist approaches all posit the existence of a small number of groups acting in cartel-like fashion, or even one group, oligopolizing or monopolizing power in the system, even where there is an apparent plurality of groups. It has been a mainstay of pluralist theory since Bentley (1908) to argue that there is a always large number of potentially significant actors in any political system, although as Truman (1951) pointed out it is important to distinguish between "organized" and "potential" (or "manifest" and "latent") groups. But in any case, the configuration of interests in traditional pluralism is always a complex one, always potentially in flux, and open to individual or particularly strategically-minded group actors – "political entrepreneurs" – to reshape or reorganize their activities to some

extent within the bounds of preexisting bargains and/or habits. But the existence of an apparent plurality of groups, as argued earlier in this chapter, is
only a necessary condition for ideal-type, competitive, self-regulating, stable
pluralism, not a sufficient one.

For ideal-type pluralism it is also crucial that groups be relatively fractionalized. This means that none is/are so much larger than the others that
they become overly dominant or hegemonic. Their clout is, if not equal, then
at least sufficient to resist domination and to be able to engage in what international relations theorists call "balancing" behavior, i.e. to make coalitions
to counteract the relative strength of other group(s).

Of course, groups may also engage in "bandwagoning" – coalescing with
more powerful groups – if they perceive that to be favorable to the pursuit of
their interests and/or values. This is akin to what Durkheim called a "simple
structure" (Durkheim 1949) in which there is a certain bottom line similarity
among groups – although it is not clear whether this refers to an endogenous
isomorphism or merely analogous exogenous characteristics or behavior
(Waltz [1979] is never entirely clear on this, although he tends towards the
latter) – as distinct from a "complex structure", in which there is a division of
labor among groups, systematically differentiating them by function – and
therefore clout – within the system.

Of course, this sort of ideal-type pluralism, like perfect competition in
economics, is never realized in practice in the real world. Nevertheless, there
is an analogy here with a relatively competitive political marketplace, with its
self-stabilizing and self-regulating characteristics in principle operating to
maintain the system and to improve overall economic welfare outputs.

However, most pluralist analysts – whether theorists or empirical analysts
– tend to assume, as in Austrian economics, that pluralist politics do not exhibit automatically self-correcting tendencies towards equilibrium. Rather, as
argued earlier in this chapter, what I have called "plurality" needs to be converted or translated into relatively stable competition through institutionalized, pluralism-supporting rules of the game, embedded informal conven-
tions, and the pluralistic practices of political, economic, and social actors –
conditions that ensure a relatively high degree of competition of interests and
values in practice. Huntington and Eckstein, for example, famously argue that
non-democratic, authoritarian underlying social structures and practices are
needed in order to stabilize democratic political systems. Dahl (1972) and
Lindblom (1977) do not go quite so far, but do suggest in their notion of
neo-pluralism that balanced, fractionalized pluralism is rarely if ever found
in the real world. Some groups are always "more equal than others" in the
Orwellian sense of the term, possessing greater resources and the ability to
deploy them tactically and strategically in systematic ways over time, locking
in a certain hegemony.

Nevertheless, unlike elitism, class analysis, and most forms of neo-corporatism – although Schmitter (1974) is ambiguous on this, as his "liberal corporatism" is pluralistic up to a point – pluralism, including neopluralism, does suggest that control of policy outcomes even in relatively oligopolistic and monopolistic political systems is always vulnerable to coalitions of outsiders, or of outsiders aligned with sub-groups of insiders. The issue is not one of a clear demarcation between pluralism and non-pluralism, but of a scale from an ideal-type political monopoly or monism (never entirely realized in practice despite the concept of totalitarianism, as historians of Stalinism and the Third Reich have shown), at one end of the spectrum, to ideal-type competitive, fractionalized pluralism at the other end.

Thus the base is always skewed, even in pluralist analysis, despite a certain underlying normative bias towards more competitive forms as the best substitute for (also non-achievable) ideal-type democracy. Actors are thus never free of underlying structural constraints although they do have a certain autonomy and ability to exert direct or indirect influence in a *relatively* pluralized context through the practices that constitute governmentality.

B. Intermediaries

Whether one is talking about "the state" in the strict sense of modern, domestic nation-state political systems or a wider category of "state-like" structures, the key question for pluralism is whether such structures are relatively *open* or *closed*. The plural base, as outlined above, concerns the "raw material" of pluralism – the configuration of interests and political market actors that constitute and generate inputs into a political system.

However, those inputs never arrive in their original form. They are translated, reshaped and transformed into resources or currency that can be used, manipulated and exchanged within the system itself. The main circuit of transformation consists of relations between formal and informal representatives of the different interests that comprise the base, whether politicians, pressure groups, latent categories of voters, protestors, or whatever, on the one hand, and politicians and bureaucrats in their official capacities, along with other members of policy communities and other well-connected influentials or "notables", on the other. Of course political officials fall into both categories, as they would be expected to do in a representative liberal democracy, and as they do in practice in other types of political system as well.

These relationships often take the form of networks. They are sometimes said to produce certain types of "withinputs", i.e. coming somewhere between inputs and outputs. (Our next category, below, institutionalized playing fields, constitutes another kind of classic withinput in political systems analysis.) These networks can be either relatively open or closed, as noted above. Ideal-type pluralism requires that networks be relatively open, i.e. that the transformation of inputs into withinputs and relationships between their members across the "input/withinput" divide be relatively transparent and open to competition, new entrants, and straightforward bargaining. Many of the more closed patterns identified by political sociologists have been more relevant to the nation-state level, including neocorporatism, private interest governments, and the corporate state.

However, others, including policy communities and networks, epistemic communities, transnational elites, transgovernmental networks, civil society, the power of financial market actors and multinational corporations, and actors within cross-border institutional structures such as "international regimes", "global governance" processes, etc., have a wider application and are at the heart of the globalization/pluralization nexus.

C. Institutional Superstructures

A great deal of attention has been paid in the international relations and international political economy literature to institutional changes linked with globalization, especially through the concept of "multilevel governance". This institutionalist approach looks not so much at actors as at structures, but paradoxically it too focuses on a kind of institutional pluralism (or even institutional schizophrenia).

We argued earlier in this chapter that pluralism is mutually constituted by the interaction of a plurality of groups and the existence or construction of a pluralism-supporting playing field, mediated by a range of actors engaging in various pluralistic and/or quasi-pluralistic practices. In this sense, the pluralization/globalization nexus is inextricably linked with the coexistence and multilayered interaction of not just national states and traditional international institutions, but also various regimes and governance institutions, transnational linkages and networks, local and regional institutions (whether subnational/regional like cities or development zones, or international/regional like free trade areas and the European Union), private regimes and webs of governance, etc.

The world cities literature, in particular, refers to the "rescaling of statehood" (Brenner 2004) above, below, and cutting across the level of the nation-state, which then becomes enmeshed in overlapping "webs of governance" (Cerny 2002). Thus the changing institutional superstructure embodies a growing institutional plurality that plural, strategically selective actors may or may not be able to manage or reshape in ways that reinforce or generate pluralism on a global or transnational scale.

VII. Globalization as Constituting Permissive Conditions for Pluralism

The most perplexing aspect of globalization is its complexity. Analysts have identified a range of dimensions of this complexity. In the first place, globalization involves transnational interpenetration, or the violation and undermining of the "inside/outside" distinction with regard to the nation-state. Furthermore, it involves the reconstitution of the public-private divide. With the notion of "publicness" being historically associated with the nation-state and "economic" institutions and processes being identified as essentially "private" (despite the crucial economic role of states), globalization is often seen, particularly by "anti-globalization" critics, as reinforcing the role of actors primarily concerned with pursuing their private (and antisocial?) economic interests to the detriment of the common good or public interest.

Although some writers talk about the emergence of a global "public sphere" (Germain 2001), the main thrust of the literature on globalization is that globalization makes such publicness more problematic – creating a need for a new politics of reshaping multi-level governance around various "new architectures" that will recreate the "public" either at a higher level or through a more complex network structure.

At the same time, however, as noted earlier, globalization also involves the uneven multiplication of points of access and control, which, allied with plurality, pluralistic practices, and pluralism-promoting strategic actors, might involve the evolution of a new kind of global pluralism, however uneven.

A. The Base: Monopoly or Competition?

In this context, what is happening with the base, or the "exogenous independent variables" identified by Spruyt? Do such changes support genuine competitive pluralization, or do they merely entrench new forms of political oligopoly or monopoly at a transnational and/or global level? In the global economy, shifting patterns with regard to economies of scale and scope do not provide conclusive evidence either way. Of course, multinational corporations hold a "privileged position", as do financial market actors in an integrated, 24-hour global financial marketplace.

But small and medium-sized enterprises also increasingly operate on a transnational scale, and it is even argued that globalization is leading to a long-term Ricardian process of the equalization of wages in the world (Kitching 2001). Only where particular industries such as commercial aircraft manufacturing, possess overwhelmingly global economies of scale are oligopoly and monopoly clearly winning (usually with state support), whereas in nearly every other industry new entrants have been proliferating. Of course, "old groups" have in many cases been able to parlay their existing resources into new profits by developing new investment strategies, restructuring and "flexibilizing" enterprises, etc.

Perhaps more important, however, has been the emergence of "new" groups of entrepreneurs, whether in countries that have traditionally supported such groups like the United States or in those that have in the past suppressed or inhibited their activities, like China and India. The power of latent or potential groups or categories has been growing as well. Perhaps the most important of these is consumers, whose role in the allocation of resources has dramatically increased in contrast with that of more traditional producer groups.

Of course, new categories of losers have been created as well, although in many cases these are groups that have long been disenfranchised, suppressed, or subsumed in authoritarian social hierarchies, such as tribes. Existing hierarchies are everywhere being challenged by new coalitions, whether coalitions seeking greater participation in global capitalism and economic growth or those seeking to resist change such as traditional kinship hierarchies, anticapitalist movements, or religious fundamentalists.

B. Intermediaries: Complex Networks

A dialectic of fractionalization and reorganization is therefore taking place that is analogous to the "restructuring of socio-political coalitions" that Spruyt identified with regard to the earlier transition from feudalism to the nation-state. The control of politics by preexisting iron triangles, corporatist blocs, or domestic policy coalitions is everywhere being challenged by different coalitions at different levels of aggregation and organization.

Perhaps the most important change in developed countries has been the growing predominance in economic policymaking of transnationally linked interest and value groups and the decline of nationally-based, protectionist politics. While it is always possible for geographically concentrated groups whose position is worsened by economic globalization, such as workers displaced by import competition or by outsourcing, to organize resistance up to a point – and often to receive media attention for doing so – the increasing imbrication of both small and large businesses in international markets, production chains and strategic alliances has tended to diffuse such effects more widely across the economy. Together with the combination of deskilling and reskilling of the workforce, along with the flexibilization of production methods and the long-term decline of trade unions, it is becoming more and more difficult to organize politically effective resistance.

Meanwhile the restructuring of financial markets has drawn more sectors of the population into marketized finance, whether directly or through institutional investors such as pension funds, while traditional banking institutions have themselves become more marketized. In other words, the socio-political balance between what were once called "national capital" and "international capital" has both blurred and shifted, as there is little purely national capital left.

The blurring of these traditional lines between what once formed the basis for the left-right divide at national level has switched the focus of group politics toward other kinds of linkages – whether the translocal restructuring of influence around multiculturalism and/or mutually exclusive but cross-border religious and ethnic identities, diaspora communities, world cities, and the like, on the one hand, or the transnational/global reorganizing of businesses and market structures around more extended networks, the development of epistemic communities of scientists and experts, the rapid growth of transnational advocacy coalitions and networks (NGOs, civil society, environmentalism, etc.), on the other.

Certain dimensions of public and economic policy have increasingly become embedded and overdetermined – the reduction of barriers to trade and cross-border finance, the shift of government policy away from direct intervention toward regulation, the transformation of the state from the welfare state to the competition state, the expansion of mixed governance and the outsourcing of traditional governmental functions to private and/or mixed public/private providers, the flexibilization of labor markets, etc. – constitute a new "embedded neoliberalism" (Soederberg Menz, and Cerny 2006). And across borders, more and more policy issue areas are debated and competed over in various mixed arenas of transnational regimes and global governance.

As noted earlier, actors must themselves be able to operate on the basis of flexible response, shifting coalition-building, and variable geometry in terms of both choosing short-term and/or long-term allies and developing policy strategies that involve the coordination of policymaking across borders. Long-term left/right blocs are giving way to mixed, complex, and shifting coalitions. Indeed, this process is running well ahead of consciousness of the implications of such changes, leading to political cognitive dissonance and, at times, to strange alliances that distort preferences rather than effectively pursuing them (Frank 2004).

C. The Superstructure: Regimes, Governance and Complexity

As stated before, this kind of political transformation has led to a range of new debates, and not a few confusions, concerning the nature of the superstructural complex that is evolving – and being continually shaped and reshaped by actors. Pluralism is particularly relevant to a context where institutional parameters are in flux; it is, after all, as Bentley (1908) contended, itself a "great moving process".

Probably the central debate has been about the role of the state. Despite all of the debate about the "hollowing out of the state", for example, it is still clear that the nation-state remains the most durable and strongly organized institutional structure in the world (Cerny 1990, 1999b; Jessop 2002). Little can be achieved politically without the nation-state.

But in many ways, the state itself can do less (Strange 1996) – or at least the state is increasingly led to do things differently. Its role is being transformed as different demands are made and different outcomes are seen to be relevant. For example, in the making of economic policy, treasuries are more limited by what they can do in an era of tax cuts, while central banks, with their relative independence from "political" control and their close links to international financial markets, are increasingly the source of the most important decisions not only for the national economy but also for the global economy. The shift of the core of policymaking and policy outputs from redistribution to regulation, noted earlier, has, paradoxically, meant the construction and imposition of increasingly restrictive and hierarchical regulatory regimes (Moran 2003). The "agencification" of national, subnational/regional, and local governance has created new spaces for special interests to inhabit and capture.

But control of the state no longer means the control of policy outcomes, as the multiplication of levels of governance leads not so much to a more effective division of labor among decisionmakers and decision-implementers as to a multiplication of sites of conflict, competition, and coalition-building. This kind of institutional schizophrenia makes it more difficult for groups to act strategically, as they must be continually rethinking and reorganizing their strategies and tactics – not to mention their internal organizations and external alliances. Nevertheless, this involves a learning curve, and the literatures on global civil society and global governance essentially focus on that learning curve, even if mainly from an institutional-determinist perspective rather than from an actor-oriented one. The development of multi-nodal politics is both an existing reality and a pluralist project in the making.

VIII. The Mutual Constitution of Globalization and Pluralization

Pluralism is *plastic*. The number, character, and configuration of groups changes shape and *modus operandi* depending upon the configuration of rewards and penalties, constraints and opportunities characterizing the predominant playing field – institutions, processes, and practices – or what Crozier and Friedberg called the "structured field of action" of politics (Crozier and Friedberg 1977).

At the same time, actors none the less have a certain both manifest and potential strategic as well as tactical autonomy in seeking to modify, tinker with or fundamentally alter that playing field. The changing constellation of actors in a globalizing world plus the increasing complexity of the structured field of action creates opportunities for reactively and/or proactively restructuring that playing field itself as particular problems and issues are confronted in practice, at all levels – micro, meso and macro. This process not only gives political entrepreneurs more scope for action but also creates openings and spaces within which institutional entrepreneurs are likely to attempt strategic restructuring. New patterns of influence and control are generated – not merely fractionalization, but also new hierarchies, control mechanisms and unequal power structures. In a globalizing world, some get more than others, while new patterns of rewards and penalties, etc., lead to attempts to innovate in patterns of coalition-building, competition and conflict.

In the meantime, the state, along with all the other emerging levels of political interaction, decisionmaking, and implementation, remains, as in pluralist theory, less the reified source of policies and outcomes in and of itself, and more a terrain or site of conflict and coalition-building as competing groups, old and new, attempt to come to terms with the implications of politics in a transnationally interpenetrated world.

Perhaps the most significant feature of pluralism as a paradigmatic concept is that it is not static. Unlike theories of politics based on domination or consensus for its own sake, it involves a great moving process. Of course, its ideal-type form is fragile, because it is never realized in practice and depends upon political practices and institutional rules of the game for its stabilization and continuity.

At the same time, however, it is inherently dynamic and the very plurality of groups in a changing structural context gives it a critical fungibility in a world in flux. In this context, actors are the link that makes plurality pluralistic – or constrains it from being so. Just as Adam Smith argued that getting two or three businessmen together in the same room is likely to lead to a conspiracy against the public interest, it is of course only to be predicted that political actors are likely to engage in monopolistic behavior much, if not all, of the time. But pluralism is also normatively necessary for the pursuit of wider interests, for the pursuit of political stability, economic growth, and social development – what has been called "enlightened self-interest".

New coalition-building opportunities, the rethinking of the substance of interests by key actors, and attempts by political and institutional entrepreneurs to innovate and shape the emerging structured field of action give those actors a kind of potential strategic institution-building role analogous to that which characterized earlier periods of historical organizational change such as the transition from feudalism to capitalism, the consolidation of the nation-state and the international states system, and the spread of mass politics, bureaucracy and liberal democracy characteristic of structural trends, from the 15th to the 20th centuries.

At the same time, opportunities for shaping change today are unprecedented because of the complexity of the institutional structure of a globalizing world added to the internationalization, transnationalization, and translocalization of networks and webs of governance and the uneven pluralization of the group universe itself. Globalization is both the source and the product of pluralization, and *vice-versa*; they are mutually constituted, and that is what gives both of them together a new dynamic potential for shaping change.

Processes of change will not be smooth or self-regulating; there will be the development of new inequalities, conflicts and destabilizing events, interacting with old inequalities, conflicts and destabilizing events in a heady brew represented in its more extreme form by cross-border ethnic and religious conflicts and terrorism. Paradoxically and for this very reason, pluralism's structural plasticity along with the skills of political and institutional entrepreneurs puts it at the heart of the action. Whether what emerges is a messy continuation of neo-medievalism (Cerny 2000c), or something more structurally integrated and culturally holistic, is in question.

In this uneven, complex, transnationalizing world, globalization is increasingly what actors make of it – and there is a very wide range of policy outcomes, types of political institutions, processes and practices potentially available to effective political entrepreneurs and the coalitions they may construct and entrench as the 21st century unfolds.

Bibliography

Almond, Gabriel A., and Verba, Sidney 1965: *The Civic Culture: Political Attitudes and Democracy in Five Nations*, Boston: Little Brown

Anderson, Benedict 1983: *Imagined Communities: Reflections on the Origin and Spread of Nationalism*, London: Verso

Apter, David E. 1977: *Introduction to Political Analysis*, Cambridge: Winthrop

Archard, David, and Macleod, Colin, eds. 2002: *The Moral and Political Status of Children*, Oxford: Oxford University Press

Bader, Veit 2001: "Culture and Identity: Contesting Constructivism", *Ethnicities* 1:2 (August), 277–299

———— 2005: "Associative Democracy and Minorities within Minorities", in: Eisenberg, Avigail, and Spinner-Halev, Jeff, eds.: *Minorities within Minorities*, Cambridge: Cambridge University Press, 319–339

Barker, Ernest 1950: "Introduction" to Otto von Gierke, *Natural Law and the Theory of Sovereignty 1500–1800*, Vol. 1. Ernest Barker ed. and transl., Cambridge: Cambridge University Press

———— 1958: *Reflections on Government*, New York: Oxford University Press

Barnes, Harry Elmer 1921: "Some Contributions of Sociology to Modern Political Theory", *American Political Science Review* XV, 487–533

Barry, Brian 2001: *Culture and Equality*, Cambridge: Harvard University Press

Beer, Samuel H. 1975: "Introduction", in: Webb, Sidney, and Webb, Beatrice, eds.: *A Constitution for the Socialist Commonwealth of Great Britain*, London: Longmans, Green, IX–XXXIII

Bell, Daniel 1960: *The End of Ideology*, Glencoe, Ill.: Free Press

Bellamy, Richard 1999: *Pluralism and Liberalism*, London/New York: Routledge

Bellamy, Richard, and Hollis, Martin 1999: "Consensus, Neutrality and Compromise", in: Bellamy and Hollis, eds., *Pluralism and Liberal Neutrality*, Portland: Frank Cass, 54–78

Bentley, Arthur F. 1908: *The Process of Government*. Chicago: University of Chicago Press

Berelson, Bernard R.; Lazarsfeld, Paul F., and McPhee, William 1954: *Voting: A Study of Opinion Formation in a Presidential Campaign*, Chicago: University of Chicago Press

Berlin, Isaiah 1990: *The Crooked Timber of Humanity: Chapters in the History of Ideas*, Hardy, Henry, ed., London: John Murray

Bermbach, Udo, and Nuscheler, Franz, eds. 1973: *Sozialistischer Pluralismus*, Hamburg: Hoffmann & Campe

Betsill, Michele M. 1999: "Changing the Climate: NGOs, Norms and the Politics of Global Climate Change", paper delivered at the Annual Convention of the International Studies Association, Washington, DC, 16–20 February

Beyme, Klaus von 1979: "Der Neo-Korporatismus und die Politik des begrenzten Pluralismus in der Bundesrepublik, in: Habermas, Jürgen, ed.: *Stichworte zur 'Geistigen Situation der Zeit'*, Frankfurt: Suhrkamp, 229–247

Blanke, Bernhard; Jürgens, Ulrich, and Kastendiek, Hans 1975: *Kritik der Politischen Wissenschaft*, Vol. 1, Frankfurt: Campus

Boudon, Raymond, and Bourricaud, François 1989: *A Critical Dictionary of Sociology*, Chicago: University of Chicago Press

Brady, David W., and Volden, Craig 1998: *Revolving Gridlock – Politics and Policy from Carter to Clinton*, Boulder: Westview Press

Brand, Donald 1988: *Corporatism and the Rule of Law*, Ithaca: Cornell University Press

Brenner, Neil 2004: *New State Spaces: Urban Governance and the Rescaling of Statehood*, Oxford/New York: Oxford University Press

Burchell, Graham; Gordon, Colin, and Miller, Peter, eds. 1991: *The Foucault Effect: Studies in Governmentality*, Chicago: University of Chicago Press

Burke, Edmund 1790: *Reflections on the Revolution in France*, Reprint. Indianapolis: Liberty Fund Edition

Calise, Mauro, and Lowi, Theodore J. 2000: "Hyperpolitics: Hypertext, Concepts and Theory-Making", *International Political Science Review* 21, 283–310

———— 2003: "Hyperpolitics: Making Political Science Research in the Web Environment", *European Political Science*, 27–40

Campbell, Angus; Converse, Philip E.; Miller, Warren E., and Stokes, Donald E. 1964: *The American Voter: An Abridgement*, New York: John Wiley and Sons

Cerny, Philip G. 1990: *The Changing Architecture of Politics: Structure, Agency, and the Future of the State*, London: Sage

———— 1995: "Globalization and the Changing Logic of Collective Action," *International Organization* 49, 595–625

———— 1997: "Paradoxes of the Competition State: The Dynamics of Political Globalization", *Government and Opposition* 32, 251–274

———— 1999a: "Globalization and the Erosion of Democracy", *European Journal of Political Research* 36, 1–26

———— 1999b: "Reconstructing the Political in a Globalizing World: States, Institutions, Agency and Governance", in: Buelens, Frans, ed.: *Globalization and the Nation-State*, Cheltenham/Northampton: Edward Elgar, 89–137

———— 2000a: "Political Agency in a Globalizing World: Toward a Structurational Approach," *European Journal of International Relations* 6, 435–464

———— 2000b: "Globalization and the Restructuring of the Political Arena: Paradoxes of the Competition State," in: Randall Germain, ed.: *Globalization and Its Critics: Perspectives from Political Economy*, London: Macmillan, 117–138

———— 2000c: "Globalization and the Disarticulation of Political Power: Toward a New Middle Ages?", in: Goverde, Henri; Cerny, Philip G.; Haugaard, Mark, and Lentner, Howard H., eds.: *Power in Contemporary Politics: Theories, Practices, Globalizations*, London: Sage, 170–86

———— 2002: "Webs of Governance and the Privatization of Transnational Regulation", in: Andrews, David M.; Henning, C. Randall, and Pauly, Louis W., eds.: *Governing the World's Money,* Ithaca: Cornell University Press, 194–216

———— 2003a: "The Uneven Pluralization of World Politics", in: Hülsemeyer, Axel, ed.: *Globalization in the 21st Century: Convergence and Divergence*, London: Palgrave, 173–175

———— 2003b: "The Governmentalization of World Politics", paper presented at the Annual Convention of the International Studies Association, Portland, Oregon, 24 February–1 March

———— 2005: "Terrorism and the New Security Dilemma", *Naval War College Review* LVIII [58], 11–33

———— 2006: "Dilemmas of Operationalizing Hegemony", in: Haugaard, Mark, and Lentner, Howard H., eds.: *Hegemony and Power* (forthcoming)

———— forthcoming: *Multi-nodal Politics: Conflict, Competition, and Coalition-Building in a Globalizing* World (in preparation)

————, ed. 1993: *Finance and World Politics: Markets, Regimes and States in the Post-Hegemonic Era*, Aldershot/Brookfield: Edward Elgar

Coker, Francis W. 1924: "Pluralistic Theories and the Attack on State Sovereignty", in: Merriam, Charles E., and Barnes, Harry E., eds.: *A History of Political Theories*, Vol. 4, New York: Macmillan, 80–117

Cole, G. D. H. 1918: *Self-government in Industry*, London: G. Bell and Sons

———— 1920: *Social Theory*, New York: Frederick A. Stokes

Collier, David 1993: "Conceptual 'Stretching' Revisited: Adopting Categories in Comparative Analysis", *American Political Science Review* LXXXVII, 845–855

Commission of the European Communities 1976: *Die Beziehungen zwischen der EG und Portugal*, Brussels: European Communities

Connolly, William E. 1969: "The Challenge to Pluralist Theory", in Connolly, William E. (ed.): *The Bias of Pluralism*, New York: Atherton, 3–34

Coser, Lewis A. 1956: *The Functions of Social Conflict*, New York: Macmillan

Crozier, Michel, and Friedberg, Erhard 1977: *L'Acteur et le système: les contraintes de l'action collective*, Paris: Éditions du Seuil

Dahl, Robert A. 1956: *A Preface to Democratic Theory*. Chicago: University of Chicago Press

———— 1958: "Critique of the Ruling Elite Model", *American Political Science Review* 12

———— 1961: *Who Governs? Democracy and Power in an American City*, New Haven: Yale University Press

———— 1963: *Who Governs?*, New Haven/London: Yale University Press

———— 1967: *Pluralist Democracy in the United States: Conflict and Consent*, Chicago: Rand McNally

———— 1970: *After the Revolution? Authority in a Good Society*, New Haven: Yale University Press

———— 1972: *Polyarchy: Participation and Opposition*, New Haven: Yale University Press

———— 1978: "Pluralism Revisited", *Comparative Politics* 10, 191–203

———— 1982: *Dilemmas of Pluralist Democracy*, New Haven: Yale University Press

———— 1986: *Democracy, Liberty, and Equality*, Oslo: Norwegian University Press

———— 1989: *Democracy and Its Critics*, New Haven: Yale University Press

Dahl, Robert A., and Lindblom, Charles E. 1953: *Politics, Economics and Welfare*, Chicago: Chicago University Press

———— 1976: "Preface", in: Re-Issue of Dahl, and Lindblom, op. cit., XXI–XLIV

Deane, Harold A. 1955: *The Political Ideas of Harold J. Laski*, New York: Columbia University Press

Detjen, Joachim 1988: *Neopluralismus und Naturrecht*, Paderborn: Schöningh

Dewey, John 1927, *The Public and its Problems,* NY: Henry Holt and Co.

Downs, Anthony 1957: *An Economic Theory of Democracy*, New York: Harper & Rowe

Dulles, Foster Rhea, and Dubovsky, Melvin 1993: *Labor in America – A History*, Arlington Heights: Harlan Davidson

Durando, Dario 1993: "The Rediscovery of Identity", *Telos*, No. 97, 117–144

Durkheim, Emile 1949: *The Division of Labor in Society*, New York: Free Press

Duverger, Maurice 1951: *Political Parties: Their Organization and Activity in the Modern State*, New York: John Wiley

Easton, David 1953: *The Political System: An Inquiry into the State of Political Science*, New York: Alfred A. Knopf

———— 1969: "The New Revolution in Political Science", *American Political Science Review* LXIII, 1051–1061

Eckstein, Harry 1965: *A Theory of Stable Democracy*, Princeton, NJ: Center for International Studies

———— 1966: *Division and Cohesion in Democracy*, Princeton: Princeton University Press

Edwards, Michael 2004: *Civil Society*, Cambridge: Polity Press

Ehrenberg, John 1999: *Civil Society: The Critical History of an Idea*, New York: New York University Press

Einaudi, Mario; Byé, Maurice, and Rossi, Ernesto 1955: *Nationalization in France and Italy*, Ithaca, NY: Cornell University Press

Eisenberg, Avigail E. 1995: *Reconstructing Political Pluralism*, Albany: SUNY Press

Eisfeld, Rainer 1972: *Pluralismus zwischen Liberalismus und Sozialismus*, Stuttgart: Kohlhammer

———— 1986: "Pluralism as a Critical Political Theory", *Praxis International* 6, 277–293

———— 1996: "The Emergence and Meaning of Socialist Pluralism", *International Political Science Review* 17, 267–279

———— 1998: "From Hegelianism to Neo-pluralism: the Uneasy Relationship between Private and Public Interest in Germany", *International Review of Sociology* 8, 389–396

Ellis, Ellen D. 1923: "Guild Socialism and Pluralism", *American Political Science Review* XVII, 584–596

Ellis, R. J. 2001: "Pluralism", in: *International Encyclopedia of the Social & Behavioral Sciences*, Vol. 17, eds. Smelser, Neil J., and Baltes, Paul B., New York: Elsevier, 11516–11520.

Engelstad, Fredrik, and Østerud, Øyvind, eds. 2004: *Power and Democracy*, Aldershot: Ashgate

Etzioni, Amitai 1968: *The Active Society*, London/New York: Free Press

Figgis, John Neville 1913: *Churches in the Modern State,* London: Longmans, Green and Co.

Follett, Mary P. 1918: *The New State*, New York: Longmans, Green and Co.

Fontana, Benedetto 1993: *Hegemony and Power: On the Relation between Gramsci and Machiavelli*, Minneapolis: University of Minnesota Press

———— 2006: "Liberty and Domination: Civil Society in Gramsci", *Boundary 2*, Vol. 33, No. 2 (Summer)

Fontana, Benedetto; Nederman, Cary J., and Remer, Gary 2004: "Introduction: Deliberative Democracy and the Rhetorical Turn", in: Fontana, Benedetto; Nederman, Cary J., and Remer, Gary, eds.: *Talking Democracy: Historical Perspectives on*

Rhetoric and Democracy, University Park: Pennsylvania State University Press, 1–56

Fraenkel, Ernst 1957: "Pluralismus", in: Fraenkel, Ernst, and Bracher, Karl Dietrich, eds.: *Fischer Lexikon Staat und Politik*, Frankfurt: S. Fischer, 234–236

——— 1964: *Der Pluralismus als Strukturelement der freiheitlich-rechtsstaatlichen Demokratie*, Munich: C. H. Beck

——— 1968: *Deutschland und die westlichen Demokratien*, Stuttgart: Kohlhammer

——— 1973: "Anstatt einer Vorrede", in: Fraenkel, Ernst, *Reformismus und Pluralismus*, Falk Esche, and Frank Grube, eds., Hamburg: Hoffmann & Campe, 11–26

Frank, Thomas 2004: *What's the Matter with Kansas? How the Conservatives Won the Heart of America*, New York: Metropolitan Books

Friedrich, Carl J. 1932: Introduction, in: Althusius, Johannes: *Politica Methodice Digesta*, Cambridge: Harvard University Press, XV-XCIX

——— 1968: *Constitutional Government and Democracy*, Waltham: Blaisdell

Furnivall, J. S. 1948: *Colonial Policy and Practice,* New York: New York University Press

Galbraith, John Kenneth 1956: *American Capitalism. The Concept of Countervailing Power*, Boston: Houghton Mifflin

Galeotti, Anna Elisabetta 1999: "Neutrality and Recognition", in: Bellamy, and Hollis, eds., op. cit., 37–53

Galston, William 1999: "Expressive Liberty, Moral Pluralism, Political Pluralism: three sources of liberal theory", *William and Mary Law Review* 40: 869–907

——— 2002: *Liberal Pluralism*, Cambridge/New York: Cambridge University Press

Garrett, Geoffrey 1998: *Partisan Politics in the Global Economy*, Cambridge/New York: Cambridge University Press

Garson, G. David 1978: *Group Theories of Politics*, Beverly Hills/London: Sage

Germain, Randall 2001: "Global Financial Governance and the Problem of Inclusion", *Global Governance* 7, 411–26

Gettell, Raymond G. 1924: *History of Political Thought*, London: Allen

Giddens, Anthony 1979: *Central Problems in Social Theory: Action, Structure and Contradiction in Social Analysis*, London: Macmillan

Gierke, Otto von 1977: *Associations and Law: The Classical and Early Christian Stages*, George Heiman ed. and transl., Toronto: University of Toronto Press

Glazer, Nathan 1997: "Individual Rights against Group Rights", in: Kymlicka, Will, ed., op. cit., 123–138

Glazer, Nathan, and Moynihan, Daniel P., eds. 1975: *Ethnicity*, Cambridge/London: Harvard University Press

Gordon, Milton M. 1975: "Toward a General Theory of Racial and Ethnic Group Relations", in: Glazer, and Moynihan, eds., op. cit., 84–110

——— 1981: "Models of Pluralism. The New American Dilemma", in: id., ed.: *America as a Multicultural Society*, Annals of the American Academy of Political and Social Science, Vol. 454, 178–188

Goulbourne, Harry 1991: "Varieties of Pluralism: The Notion of a Pluralist Post-Imperial Great Britain", *New Community*, Vol. 17, 211–227

Greenberg, Edward S. 1981: "Industrial Self-Management and Political Attitudes", *American Political Science Review* LXXV, 29–42

Gundersheimer, Werner 1981: "Patronage and the Renaissance: An Exploratory Approach", in: Lytle, Guy Fitch, and Orgel, Stephen, eds.: *Patronage in the Renaissance*, Princeton: Princeton University Press, 3–23

Gunnell, John G. 1993: *The Descent of Political Theory: The Geneology of an American Vocation*, Chicago: University of Chicago Press

———— 2004: *Imagining the American Polity*, University Park: Pennsylvania University Press

Gutmann, Amy 2003: *Democracy and Identity*, Princeton: Princeton University Press

Hall, Peter A., and Taylor, Rosemary C. M. 1996: "Political Science and the Three New Institutionalisms", *Political Studies* 44, 936–57

Hallowell, John H. 1943: *The Decline of Liberalism as an Ideology*, Berkeley: University of California Press

Haugaard, Mark 2003: "Reflections on Seven Ways of Creating Power", *European Journal of Social Theory* 6, 87–113

Heiman, George 1977: "Introduction" to Gierke, op. cit., 1–68

———— 1993: "Associational Democracy", in Held, David, ed., *Prospects for Democracy: North, South, East, West*, Cambridge, UK: Polity Press

Held, David 2003: *Models of Democracy*, Cambridge/Oxford: Polity/Blackwell

Hirsch, Fred 1976: *Social Limits to Growth*, Cambridge: Harvard University Press

Hirst, Paul 1993: *Associative Democracy*, Cambridge: Polity Press

———— 2004: "What is Globalization?", in: Engelstad, and Østerud, op. cit., 151–168

Huntington, Samuel P. 1968: *Political Order in Changing Societies*, New Haven: Yale University Press

Hymer, Stephen, and Rowthorn, Robert 1970: "Multinational Corporations and International Oligopoly", in: Kindleberger, Charles P. (ed.): *The International Corporation*, Cambridge: M.I.T. Press, 57–91

Ionescu, Ghita 1975: *Centripetal Politics: Government and the New Centres of Power*, London: Hart-Davis

James, Matt, forthcoming: *Misrecognized Materialists: Social Movements in Canadian Constitutional Politics*, Vancouver: University of British Columbia Press

James, William 1909: *A Pluralistic Universe*, New York: Longmans, Green

Jessop, Bob 1979: "Corporatism, Parliamentarism and Social Democracy", in: Schmitter, and Lehmbruch, eds., op. cit., 185–212

———— 2002: *The Future of the Capitalist State*, Cambridge: Polity Press

Johnson, James 2000: "Why Respect Culture?", in: *American Journal of Political Science* 44, 405–18

Kallen, Horace M. 1915: "Democracy Versus the Melting-Pot", *Nation* 100, 190–194, 217–220

———— 1924: *Culture and Democracy in the United States*, New York: Boni & Liveright

———— 1956: *Cultural Pluralism and the American Dream*, Philadelphia: University of Pennsylvania Press

Katzenstein, Peter 1985: *Small States in World Markets*, Ithaca: Cornell University Press

Keck, Margaret E., and Sikkink, Kathryn 1998: *Activists Beyond Borders: Advocacy Networks in International Politics*, Ithaca: Cornell University Press

Kitching, Gavin 2001: *Seeking Social Justice Through Globalization: Escaping a Nationalist Perspective*, University Park: Pennsylvania State University Press

Kolko, Gabriel 1963: *The Triumph of Conservatism. A Reinterpretation of American History, 1900–1916*, Glencoe, Ill.: Free Press

Kornhauser, William 1961: *The Politics of Mass Society*, Glencoe, Ill.: Free Press

Kramnick, Isaac, and Sheerman, Barry 1993: *Harold Laski: A Life on the Left*, New York: Penguin

Kremendahl, Hans 1977: *Pluralismustheorie in Deutschland*, Leverkusen: Heggen

Kuhn, Thomas S. 1962: *The Structure of Scientific Revolutions*, 2nd ed., Chicago: University of Chicago Press

Kukathas, Chandran 1997: "Are there any Cultural Rights?", in: Kymlicka, Will, ed., op. cit., 228–256

———— 2003: *The Liberal Archipelago*, Oxford: Oxford University Press

Kuper, Leo 1969: "Plural Societies: Perspectives and Problems", in: Kuper, Leo, and Smith, M. G., eds.: *Pluralism in Africa*, Berkeley and Los Angeles: University of California Press, 7–26

Kymlicka, Will 1995: *Multicultural Citizenship*, Oxford/New York: Clarendon Press

———— ed. 1997: *The Rights of Minority Cultures*, Oxford/New York: Oxford University Press

Laski, Harold J. 1917: *Studies in the Problem of Sovereignty*, New Haven: Yale University Press

———— 1919a: "The Pluralistic State", *The Philosophical Review* 28 (November)

———— 1919b: *Authority in the Modern State*, New Haven: Yale University Press

———— 1921: *The Foundations of Sovereignty and Other Essays,* New York/London: Harcourt, Brace

———— 1923: "Canada's Constitution", *The New* Republic 35 (4 July)

———— 1925: *A Grammar of Politics*, Reprint 1948. London: George Allen & Unwin

Lasswell, Harold D. 1950: *Politics: Who Gets What, When, How*, Gloucester: Peter Smith

Latham, Earl 1952: *The Group Basis of Politics*, Ithaca: Cornell University Press

Lazarsfeld, Paul F.; Berelson, Bernard, and Gaudet, Hazel ^{2}1948: *The People's Choice*, New York: Columbia University Press

Lehmbruch, Gerhard 1979: "Liberal Corporatism and Party Government", in: Schmitter, and Lehmbruch, op. cit., 147–183

Levi-Faur, David, and Jordana, Jacinta, eds. 2005: *The Rise of Regulatory Capitalism: The Global Diffusion of a New Order*, Annals of the American Academy of Political and Social Science, No. 598, London: Sage

Levy, Jacob 2005: "Sexual Orientation, Exit and Refuge", in: Eisenberg, Avigail, and Spinner-Halev, Jeff, eds.: *Minorities within Minorities,* Cambridge: Cambridge University Press

Lichtenstein, Nelson 2002: *State of the Union – A Century of American Labor*, Princeton: Princeton University Press

Lijphart, Arend 1968: *The Politics of Accommodation*, Berkeley/Los Angeles: California University Press

———— 1977: *Democracy in Plural Societies*, New Haven/London: Yale University Press

———— 1999: *Patterns of Democracy: Government Forms and Performance in Thirty-Six Countries*, New Haven: Yale University Press

Lindblom, Charles E. 1977: *Politics and Markets*, New York: Basic Books

Lowi, Theodore J. 1967: "The Public Philosophy: Interest-Group Liberalism", *American Political Science Review* LXI, 5–24

———— 1979: *The End of Liberalism*, New York: W. W. Norton

———— 1996: *The End of the Republican Era*, Oklahoma: University of Oklahoma Press

Lütz, S. 2004: "Convergence Within National Diversity: The Regulatory State in Finance", *Journal of Public Policy* 24, 169–197

Madison, James 1787: *The Federalist No. 10*

Maier, Charles S. 1974: "Strukturen kapitalistischer Stabilität in den zwanziger Jahren: Errungenschaften und Defekte", in: Winkler, Heinrich August, ed.: *Organisierter Kapitalismus*, Göttingen: Vandenhoeck & Ruprecht, 195–213

———— 1975: *Recasting Bourgeois Europe*, Princeton: Princeton University Press

Maine, Henry Sumner 1861: *Ancient Law*, London: J. Murray

Maitland, F. W. 1936: "Moral Personality and Legal Personality", in: Hazeltine, H. D.; Lapsley, G., and Winfield, R. H., eds., *Selected Essays*, London: Cambridge University Press

Mannheim, Karl 1929 and 1936: *Ideology and Utopia*, New York: Harcourt

Mason, Ronald M. 1982: *Participatory and Workplace Democracy*, Carbondale: Southern Illinois University Press

Mayer, Arno J. 1981: *The Persistence of the Old Regime: Europe to the Great War*, London: Croom Helm

McClelland, Charles A. 1965: "Systems Theory and Human Conflict", in: McNeil, Elton B., ed.: *The Nature of Human Conflict*, Englewood Cliffs: Prentice-Hall, 258–283

McConnell, Grant 1966: *Private Power and American Democracy*, New York: Alfred A. Knopf

McCord Wright, David 1954: "Contribution to the Discussion", *American Economic Review*, Papers & Proceedings, XLIV, 26–30

McLennan, Gregor 1995: *Pluralism*, Buckingham: Open University Press

Menand, Louis 2001: *The Metaphysical Club*, New York: Farrar, Straus & Giroux

Merelman, Richard M. 2003: *Pluralism at Yale*, Madison/London: University of Wisconsin Press

Merton, Robert 1957: *Social Theory and Social Structure*. Glencoe, Ill.: Free Press

Michels, Robert 1962: *Political Parties: A Sociological Study of the Oligarchical Tendencies of Modern Democracy*, New York: Crowell-Collier

Milbrath, Lester W. 1955: *Political Participation*, Chicago: Rand McNally

Mill, John Stuart 1975: "Considerations on Representative Government", in: Mill, John Stuart: *Three Essays*, Oxford/New York: Oxford University Press

Mills, C. Wright 1963: "Liberal Values in the Modern World", in: Mills, C. Wright: *Power, Politics and People,* New York: Ballantine Books, 187–195

Mitchell, William C. 1963: "Interest Group Theory and 'Overlapping Memberships': A Critique", unpubl. paper

Modood, Tariq 1999: "Multiculturalism, Secularism and the State", in: Bellamy, and Hollis, eds., op. cit., 79–97

Moran, Michael 2003: *The British Regulatory State: High Modernism and Hyper-Innovation*, Oxford: Oxford University Press

Mosca, Gaetano 1939: *The Ruling Class*, New York: McGraw Hill

New York Times 1984: "Project Democracy Takes Wing", No. 56,050, May 29, B 10

Nicholls, David 1974: *Three Varieties of Pluralism*, London: Macmillan

———— 1994: *The Pluralist State: Political Ideas of J. N. Figgis and his Contemporaries*, London: Palgrave Macmillan

Nordstrom, Carolyn 2000: "Shadows and Sovereigns", *Theory, Culture and Society* 17, 35–54

Nuscheler, Franz 1980: "Sozialistischer Pluralismus", in: Oberreuter, Heinrich, ed.: *Pluralismus*, Opladen: Leske & Budrich, 143–162

Olson, Mancur 1965: *The Logic of Collective Action*, Cambridge, MA: Harvard University Press

Orwell, George 1949: *1984*, London: Secker and Warburg

Osterberg, David, and Ajami, Fouad 1971: "The Multinational Corporation: Expanding the Frontiers of World Politics", *Journal of Conflict Resolution* 15, 457–470

Panitch, Leo 1979: "The Development of Corporatism in Liberal Democracies", in: Schmitter, and Lehmbruch, eds., op. cit., 119–146

Phillips, Anne 2004: "Democracy, Recognition and Power", in: Engelstad, and Østerup, eds., op. cit., 57–78

Putnam, Robert 2000: *Bowling Alone: The Collapse and Revival of American Community*, New York: Simon and Schuster

Putzel, James 2005: "Globalization, Liberalization, and Prospects for the State", *International Political Science Review* 26, 5–16

Réaume, Denis 1997: "Common Law Constructions of Group Autonomy: A Case Study", in: Shapiro, Ian, and Kymlicka, Will, eds.: *Ethnicity and Group Rights* (Nomos Vol. XXXIX), New York: New York University Press, 257–289

Reich, Rob 2002: *Bridging Liberalism and Multiculturalism in American Education*, Chicago: University of Chicago Press

Reitman, Oonagh 2005: "On Exit", in: Eisenberg, Avigail, and Spinner-Halev, Jeff, eds.: *Minorities within Minorities*, Cambridge: Cambridge University Press, 189–208

Ringen, Stein 2004: "Wealth and Decay. The Norwegian Study of Power and Democracy", *Times Literary Supplement*, February 13, 3–5

Rogin, Michael Paul 1967: *The Intellectuals and McCarthy: The Radical Specter*, Cambridge/London: M.I.T. Press

Rokkan, Stein 1966: "Norway: Numerical Democracy and Corporate Pluralism", in: Dahl, Robert A., ed.: *Political Opposition in Western Democracies*, New Haven: Yale University Press, 70–115

Rose, Arnold M. 1967: *The Power Structure: Political Process in American Society*, New York: Oxford University Press

Rothman, Stanley 1960: "Systematic Political Theory: Observations on the Group Approach", *American Political Science Review* LIV, 15–33

Rothschild, K. W. 1947: "Price Theory and Oligopoly", *Economic Journal* LVII, 299–320

Sabine, George 1950: *A History of Political Theory* (rev. ed.), New York: Henry Holt

Salisbury, Robert H. 1979: "Why No Corporatism in America?", in: Schmitter, and Lehmbruch, op. cit., 213–230

Sartori, Giovanni 1997: "Understanding Pluralism", *Journal of Democracy* 8, 58–69

Schiappa, Edward 2003: *Defining Reality – Definitions and the Politics of Meaning*, Carbondale: Southern Illinois University Press

Schlesinger, Arthur M. 1992: *The Disuniting of America*, New York/London: W. W. Norton

Schmitter, Philippe 1974: "Still the Century of Corporatism?", in: Pike, Frederick, and Stritch, Thomas, eds.: *The New Corporatism*, Notre Dame: Notre Dame University Press, 85–131

Schmitter, Philippe, and Lehmbruch, Gerhard, eds. 1979: *Trends Toward Corporatist Intermediation*, Beverly Hills/London: Sage

Schneiderman, David 1998: "Harold Laski, Viscount Haldane, and the Law of the Canadian Constitution in Early Twentieth Century", *University of Toronto Law Journal* 48, 521–538

Schumpeter, Joseph A. 1942: *Capitalism, Socialism, and Democracy*, New York: Harper and Row

Seidelman, Raymond 1985: *Disenchanted Realists – Political Science and the American Crisis, 1884–1984*, Albany: SUNY University Press

Simmel, Georg 1955: *Conflict and the Web of Group Affiliations*, translated by Wolff, Kurt H., and Bendix, Reinhard, New York: Free Press

Slaughter, Anne-Marie 2004: *A New World Order*, Princeton: Princeton University Press

Smith, Adam 1981: *An Inquiry Into the Nature and Causes of the Wealth of Nations*, Vol. I. Oxford: Oxford University Press

Smith, Adam 1776: *An Inquiry Into the Nature and Causes of the Wealth of Nations*, Vol. II, Reprint 1976. London: A. Strahan

Soederberg, Susanne; Menz, Georg, and Cerny, Philip G. 2002: *Internalizing Globalization: The Rise of Neoliberalism and the Erosion of National Models of Capitalism*, London: Palgrave

Spinner-Halev, Jeff 2001: "Feminism, Multiculturalism, Oppression and the State", *Ethics* 112 (1), 84–113

———— 2005: "Autonomy, Association and Pluralism", in: Eisenberg, Avigail, and Spinner-Halev, Jeff, eds.: *Minorities within Minorities*, Cambridge: Cambridge University Press, 157–171

Spruyt, Hendrik 1994: *The Sovereign State and Its Competitors: An Analysis of Systems Change*, Princeton, NJ: Princeton University Press

Stanovcic, Vojslav 1992: "Problems and Options in Institutionalizing Ethnic Relations", *International Political Science Review* 13, 359–379

Stears, Marc 2002: *Progressives, Pluralists, and the Problems of the State*, Oxford/New York: Oxford University Press

Steffani, Winfried 1980: *Pluralistische Demokratie*, Opladen: Leske & Budrich

Stigler, George J. 1954: "The Economist Plays With Blocs", *American Economic Review*, Papers & Proceedings, XLIV, 7–14

Strange, Susan 1996: *The Retreat of the State: The Diffusion of Power in the World Economy*, Cambridge: Cambridge University Press

Streeck, Wolfgang 1983: "Between Pluralism and Corporatism: German Business Associations and the State", *Journal of Public Policy* 3, 265–284

Streeck, Wolfgang, and Schmitter, Philip C., eds. 1986: *Private Interest Government: Beyond Market and State*, London: Sage

Thelen, Kathleen 1991: *Union in Parts: Labor Politics in Post-War Germany*, Ithaca: Cornell University Press

Tocqueville, Alexis de 1955: *The Old Regime and the French Revolution*, New York: Doubleday
———— 1959: *Democracy in America*. New York: Knopf, Vintage Edition
Truman, David B. 1951: *The Governmental Process*, New York: Alfred A. Knopf
Van Dyke, Vernon 1976/77: "The Individual, the State, and Ethnic Communities in Political Theory", *World Politics* XXIX, 343–369
Waldron, Jeremy 1997: "Minority Cultures and the Cosmopolitan Alternative", in: Kymlicka, Will, ed., op. cit., 93–119
Waldron, Jeremy 2000: "Cultural Identity and Civic Responsibility", in: Kymlicka, Will, and Wayne, Norman, eds.: *Citizenship in Diverse Societies*, Oxford: Oxford University Press
Waltz, K. 1979: *Theory of International Politics*, Reading: Addison-Wesley
Walzer, Michael 1997: "Pluralism: A Political Perspective", in: Kymlicka, Will, ed., op. cit., 139–154
Weber, Max 1947: *The Theory of Social and Economic Organization*, ed. Talcott Parsons, New York: Free Press
Wedel, Janine R. 2001: *Collision and Collusion – The Strange Case of Western Aid to Eastern Europe*, New York: Palgrave/St. Martin's
———— 2004: "Blurring the Boundaries of the State-Private Divide: Flex Organizations and the Decline of Accountability", in: Spoor, Max, ed.: *Globalization, Poverty and Conflict*, Boston: Kluwer, 217–235
Weinstock, Daniel 2001: "Les 'identités' sont-elles dangereuses pour la démocratie ?", in: Maclure, Jocelyn, and Gagnon, Alain-G., eds.: *Repères en mutation: Identité et citoyenneté dans le Québec contemporain*, Montréal: Éditions Québec-Amérique, 227–250
———— 2005: "Beyond Exit Rights: Reframing the Debate", in: Eisenberg, Avigail, and Spinner-Halev, Jeff, eds.: *Minorities within Minorities*, Cambridge: Cambridge University Press, 227–248
Williamson, Peter J. 1989: *Corporatism in Perspective*, London: Sage
Wright, A. W. 1974: "Guild Socialism Revisited", *Journal of Contemporary History* 9, 165–180
Young, Iris Marion 1990: *Justice and the Politics of Difference*, Princeton: Princeton University Press
Yuval-Davis, Nira 2000: "Citizenship, Territoriality and the Gendered Construction of Difference", in: Isin, E. F., ed.: *Democracy, Citizenship and the Global City*, London: Routledge, 171–188

Index

A

Affirmative action 19, 54, 77
Apathy 13, 14, 49
Austin, John 62

B

Bader, Veit 75
Bargaining 12, 13, 17, 33, 35, 37,
    44, 45, 49, 51, 52, 83, 87, 88, 89,
    104
Barker, Ernest 24, 26, 31, 62
Barnes, Harry Elmer 43, 44
Behavioralism 59
Bentley, Arthur F. 13, 16, 17, 24, 33,
    44, 45, 55, 86, 101, 108
Berlin, Isaiah 60
Brady, David 21
British Labour Party 24, 42, 44
Bryan, William Jennings 33
Burke, Edmund 28, 29
Bush, George W. 93

C

Calhoun, John C. 56
Calise, Mauro 15, 22
Capitalism 12, 16, 30, 33, 35, 39, 81,
    84, 90, 106, 110
Civil society 11, 16, 17, 25, 26, 28,
    33, 41, 81, 82, 83, 85, 95, 96, 97,
    104, 107, 108
Cleavage 25, 26, 32, 40, 55, 57, 86
Coker, Francis W. 41, 59, 67
Cold War 40, 43, 45, 46, 47
Cole, G. D. H. 13, 42, 43, 60, 62, 63,
    64, 67, 75
Competition state 20, 94, 107
Consociationalism 55

Contract 16, 27, 29, 30, 38, 48
Control 11, 13, 14, 15, 18, 39, 42,
    43, 44, 45, 47, 48, 50, 57, 76, 82,
    83, 84, 87, 88, 95, 99, 103, 105,
    106, 108, 109
Corporate hegemony 52
Corporate pluralism - *see* Pluralism
Corporation 12, 16, 17, 27, 31, 34,
    35, 36, 37, 39, 44, 48, 53, 57, 62
Corporatism 31, 34, 35, 36, 38, 51,
    52, 63, 78, 82, 87
    Liberal corporatism 14, 103
    Neo-corporatism 14, 40, 103
Countervailing power 45, 50

D

Dahl, Robert A. 13, 14, 15, 17, 18,
    25, 33, 45, 47, 48, 49, 50, 57, 59,
    60, 67, 68, 69, 71, 90, 98, 102
Democracy 3, 39, 41, 46, 69, 84
Dewey, John 44, 73
Downs, Anthony 21
Durkheim, Emile 102
Duverger, Maurice 32, 90

E

Easton, David 47, 86
Eckstein, Harry 49, 89, 92, 102
Elite 17, 25, 35, 37, 45, 49, 52, 56,
    67, 86, 87, 89, 90, 91, 92, 94, 100,
    101, 104
Elliott, William Yandall 59, 64
Ellis, Ellen Deborah 24, 28, 42, 59
Equality 43, 47, 50, 54, 66, 69
Ethnocultural pluralism
    - *see* Pluralism

F

Fabian Society 42
Faction 25, 30, 83, 87, 90
Federalism 24, 31, 55, 64, 66, 86
Feudalism 17, 28, 29, 30, 37, 99,
    106, 110
Figgis, John Neville 60, 63, 67, 72,
    79
Follett, Mary P. 12, 44, 57, 60, 73
Ford, Henry 37
Fraenkel, Ernst 12, 46, 47
Functional representation 13, 24, 42

G

Galbraith, John Kenneth 50
Giddens, Anthony 85
Gierke, Otto von 24, 62
Globalization 13, 18, 20, 30, 40, 52,
    53, 57, 81, 82, 83, 84, 85, 91, 92,
    94, 95, 96, 97, 98, 99, 100, 104,
    105, 106, 110
Gordon, Milton M. 54, 85, 89
Group rights 19, 54, 55, 63
Group theory 33
Gutmann, Amy 75, 76

H

Hirst, Paul 53, 57, 75
Hobbes, Thomas 62
Hoover, Herbert 36
Huntington, Samuel P. 33, 89, 92,
    102

I

Identity politics 60, 74, 76
Industrial self-government 14, 49
Inequality 12, 14, 49, 87
Interest group 17, 24, 25, 26, 31, 33,
    34, 35, 43, 45, 49, 68, 69, 70, 71,
    72, 73, 75, 76, 87, 99

Interest-group pluralism
    - see Pluralism
International regimes 84, 94, 104
Interventionism 12, 53

J

Jacksonian Revolution 12
James, William 22, 24, 40, 41, 54
Jessop, Bob 51, 52, 88, 99, 108
Johnson, Lyndon B. 47

K

Kallen, Horace M. 18, 54, 61
Kornhauser, William 17, 45, 49
Kuhn, Thomas S. 21
Kuthakas, Chandran 55
Kymlicka, Will 55, 56, 60, 61

L

Labour Party 13
Laski, Harold J. 13, 14, 15, 16, 17,
    18, 24, 26, 28, 39, 41, 42, 43, 44,
    48, 49, 57, 59, 60, 62, 64, 65, 66,
    67, 75, 78, 79
Latham, Earl 14, 17, 45, 48
Lehmbruch, Gerhard 51
Lenin, Vladimir I. 84
Liberal corporatism
    - see Corporatism
Liberal pluralism - see Pluralism
Liberalism 11, 21, 45, 55, 62, 83
Lijphart, Arend 36, 45, 49, 56
Lindblom, Charles 13, 14, 17, 34,
    35, 36, 45, 47, 48, 49, 57, 81, 88,
    90, 92, 98, 102
Locke, John 11

M

Madison, James 25, 27, 30, 31, 71
Maier, Charles S. 51
Maine, Henry 29

Maitland, Frederic W. 62, 72
Market 12, 14, 16, 18, 26, 27, 30, 31,
    32, 34, 37, 48, 50, 51, 52, 82, 90,
    93, 94, 95, 103, 104, 105, 107
Marx, Karl 26, 88
Marxism 24, 26, 43
McLuhan, Marshall 92
Merton, Robert K. 22, 23, 28, 32
Milbrath, Lester 17, 45
Mill, John Stuart 11, 12
Monism 19, 24, 28, 30, 46, 86, 103
Mosca, Gaetano 30
Multilevel governance 104
Multinational corporation 13, 19, 91,
    92, 104, 105

N

Neo-corporatism - *see* Corporatism
Neo-liberalism 18, 51
Neo-pluralism - *see* Pluralism
New Deal 13, 43, 44, 47
Non-governmental organizations
    (NGOs) 36, 92, 94, 107

O

Oligopoly 48, 87, 105
Overlapping membership 81
Ownership 13, 37, 43, 48

P

Participatory democracy 14, 43
Party 16, 17, 27, 29, 31, 32, 33, 35,
    37, 45, 46, 71
Patronage 16, 29, 30, 31, 88
Piaget, Jean 85
Pluralism
    Corporate pluralism 17, 51, 52, 54
        - *see also* Corporate hegemony
    Ethnocultural pluralism 18, 54
    Interest-group pluralism 69

Liberal pluralism 14, 40, 47, 49,
    50, 51, 52, 54, 55, 87
Neo-pluralism 46, 75, 98, 102
Radical pluralism 40, 48, 51
Value pluralism 60
Political resources 11, 14, 15, 18, 19,
    20, 41, 43, 49, 52, 56, 68
Polyarchy 17, 18, 24, 36, 90
Potential groups 50, 106
Poulantzas, Nicos 88
Pragmatism 41, 83
Progressivism 12, 33, 44, 66

R

Radical pluralism - *see* Pluralism
Rational choice 21, 26, 33, 34, 87
Reuther, Walter 37
Rokkan, Stein 51
Roosevelt, Franklin D. 36, 47
Rousseau, Jean-Jacques 28

S

Schlesinger, Arthur M. 40, 56
Schmitter, Philippe 36, 51, 85, 88,
    103
Schumpeter, Joseph A. 14, 40, 90
Shaw, George Bernard 33, 42
Simmel, Georg 28, 81, 86
Smith, Adam 11, 30, 31, 39, 45, 90,
    109
Social capital 38, 82, 87, 94, 96
Socialism 14
Spruyt, Hendrik 99, 100, 105, 106
Status 14, 16, 28, 29, 30, 47, 55, 56,
    57, 62, 87, 89, 95
Steffani, Winfried 46

T

Tocqueville, Alexis de 12, 13, 24,
    30, 31, 32, 92, 101
Toennies, Ferdinand 28

Totalitarianism 46, 103
Trade Unions - *see* Unions
Truman, David B. 14, 17, 25, 33, 44,
    45, 46, 47, 49, 50, 55, 81, 86, 89,
    101

U

Unions 11, 12, 14, 24, 26, 33, 34, 36,
    37, 38, 39, 42, 44, 52, 57, 62, 63,
    64, 65, 66, 71, 72, 93, 106

V

Value pluralism - *see* Pluralism

W

Webb, Beatrice 42
Webb, Sidney 42
Wedel, Janine 35, 36
Welfare state 37, 38, 93, 94, 107

Y

Young, Iris Marion 69

The World of Political Science –
The Development of the Discipline Book Series
Edited by Michael Stein and John Trent

The book series aims at going beyond the traditional "state-of-the-art review" and wants to make a major contribution not just to the description of the state of the discipline, but also to an explanation of its development and content.

Linda Shepherd (ed.)
Political Psychology
2006. 168 pp. Pb.
19.90 €/ US$ 23.95
ISBN 3-86649-027-5

The book provides detailed information about the development of the field of political psychology, a subfield of both political science and psychology. It describes the evolution of concepts and theories within political psychology, international influences in the field, current concepts and methodology, and trends that augur for the future of the enterprise.

R.B. Jain (ed.)
Governing development
across cultures
Challenges and dilemmas of an emerging sub-discipline in political science
2006. Approx. 200 pp. Pb
Approx. 19.90 €/ US$ 23.95
ISBN 3-96649-029-1

The book is a critical examination and appraisal of the status, methodology and likely future of the emerging sub-discipline of "Governing Development" within the broader discipline of political science.

David Coen & Wyn Grant (eds.)
Business and Government
Methods and Practice
2006. 127 pp. Pb. 16.90 €/ US$ 19.90
ISBN 3-86649-033-X

This volume reviews current debates on the role of business in politics and it assesses emerging methodological approaches to its study.

Verlag **Barbara Budrich**
Barbara Budrich Publishers

Head-office: Stauffenbergstr. 7 • D-51379 Leverkusen Opladen • Germany
Tel +49 (0)2171.344.594 • Fax +49 (0)2171.344.693 • info@budrich-verlag.de
US-office: 28347 Ridgebrook • Farmington Hills, MI 48334 • USA • info@barbara-budrich.net
Northamerican distribution: International Specialized Book Services
920 NE 58th Ave., suite 300 • Portland, OR 97213-3786 • USA
phone toll-free within North America 1-800-944-6190, fax 1-503-280-8832 •orders@isbs.com

www.budrich-verlag.de • www.barbara-budrich.net

Politics

Ralf Puchert
Marc Gärtner
Stephan Höyng (eds.)
Work Changes Gender
Men and Equality in the Transition of
Labour Forms. 2005. 202 pp.
Pb 19.90 €/ US$ 23.90
ISBN 3-938094-13-3
Hc 39.90 €/ US$ 48.00
ISBN 3-938094-14-1

John E. Trent
Modernizing the United Nations
System
From International Relations to Global
Governance
2006. Approx. 250 pp. Pb.
Approx. 24.90 €/ US$ 28.90
ISBN 3-86649-003-8

Ursula J. van Beek (ed.)
Democracy under Construction:
Patterns from Four Continents
2005. 500 pp. Pb 49.00 €/ US$59.90
ISBN 3-938094-23-0
Hc 79,– €/ US$ 94.90
ISBN 3-938094-24-9

Bob Reinalda
Ewa Kulesza
The Bologna Process—
Harmonizing Europe's Higher
Education
Including the essential original texts
Foreword by Hans-Dieter Klingemann
2005. XIV + 230 pp.
Pb 19.90 €/ US$ 23.90
ISBN 3-938094-39-7
Hc 48.00 €/US$ 58.00
ISBN 3-938094-53-2

 Verlag **Barbara Budrich**
Barbara Budrich Publishers

Head-office: Stauffenbergstr. 7 • D-51379 Leverkusen Opladen • Germany
Tel +49 (0)2171.344.594 • Fax +49 (0)2171.344.693 • info@budrich-verlag.de
US-office: 28347 Ridgebrook • Farmington Hills, MI 48334 • USA • info@barbara-budrich.net
Northamerican distribution: International Specialized Book Services
920 NE 58th Ave., suite 300 • Portland, OR 97213-3786 • USA
toll-free within North America ph 1-800-944-6190, fax 1-503-280-8832 • orders@isbs.com

www.budrich-verlag.de • www.barbara-budrich.net